FORGOTTEN COURAGE

CLARENCE HENDERSON
With Dr. Paul Brintley and Jason Williams

Forgotten Courage
All Rights Reserved.
Copyright © 2023 Clarence Henderson
With Jason Williams and Dr. Paul Brintley

Cover Photo © 2023 www.gettyimages.com. All rights reserved - used with permission.

PRINTED IN THE UNITED STATES OF AMERICA

Table of Contents

A Tribute to Relationship	i
Saluting a Hero	iii
Foreword	v
Chapter 1. Birth and Childhood	1
Five Influences of Your Belief	3
System Black and White	6
Two Water Fountains	8
Sports	11
Childhood Challenges	13
Injustices	18
Relationships That Defined Me	21
High School Life	24
First Year of College	26
Military Service	30
Business Engagement	33
Other Opportunities	37

Chapter 2. Family	39
Christian Faith	44
The Holy Spirit	48
Healing Through Scriptures	50
Community Service	53
Political	56
The Frederick Douglass Foundation	62
Chapter 3. Sit In	67
Agenda vs. Principle-Driven	76
Movements How Does America Work?	78
Responsibility	81
Presidentially Recognized	85
Chapter 4. Adult Life	93
Civil Rights Movement Hijacked	94
Educational System	98
Chapter 5. Life Experiences	101
Economic Empowerment	102
Anyone can be a business owner	106
Starting a Business	109
Abortion	112
Family Structure	116
The Future	119
Affirmative Action	122

Chapter 6. Projects — 123
    Content of Character™ — 124
    Program Movie project — 127

Chapter 7. Republican National Convention Speech 8/26/2020 — 129

Chapter 8. In The News (Articles and Opinions) — 133
    Grassroots Spotlight: Civil Rights Activist Clarence Henderson — 134
    Civil rights hero from 60s takes criticism as Trump backer — 137
    1960s Activist Says 'Offensive' To Equate Transgender Claims With Racial Equality — 140
    Clarence Henderson receives Order of the Long Leaf Pine — 143
    Civil Rights era demonstrator speaks on faith, unity, and God-given rights — 144
    Civil rights pioneer wants blacks to join GOP, says Democrats 'most afraid' of 'conservative blacks — 147
    Community, religious leaders gather to support charter school transportation grants — 150
    Woolworth's Protester Shares Views in Pinehurst Speech — 154
    Clarence Henderson: President Donald Trump has ended the era of broken promises by delivering real results for African Americans — 156
    President Trump Speaks At "Salute To America" Event — 159
    Two activists: conservatives are not doing enough to reach black voters — 160
    Clarence Henderson: George Floyd protests — what I learned during lunch counter sit-ins in 1960 — 164

First Woman Freed by Criminal Justice Reform Thanks
Donald Trump at Black History Month Reception   167
HENDERSON: The legacy of Dr. Martin Luther King Jr.   169
Civil Rights Hero Clarence Henderson: The future is bright
for Black North Carolinians, Just Not With 'Do Nothing
Democrats'   172
[EXCLUSIVE OP-ED] CLARENCE HENDERSON:
Biden is as good at debating as he is bad at governing   175
HENDERSON: The legacy of Dr. Martin Luther King Jr.   178
Liberal hypocrisy on full display with racist cartoon   180
HENDERSON: Are N.C. Republicans bad for
black families?   183
MENKEN/HENDERSON: Donald Trump Is Healing
The Country   186
Trump gives black Americans opportunity for greatness   191
Conservative radio host Glenn Beck leads All Lives Matter
march through Birmingham   195

Chapter 9. Our Time at the White House   197

Chapter 10. A Call to Action   201

Excerpts From Speeches   203

A TRIBUTE TO RELATIONSHIP

IT IS AN honor to stand on the same stage with Clarence Henderson. This book came to fruition because of the partnership between the NC Faith and Freedom Coalition and Clarence Henderson.

While traveling all over our state with Mr. Henderson, I was stimulated to start making notes of his speeches. I was asked by Jason Williams, the executive director of the NC Faith and Freedom Coalition, to visit local conservative organizations. Our goal is to fortify conservative values in the members of those groups. I love to inform voters of their rights and freedoms. I have the pleasure of highlighting our biblical responsibility to challenge candidates to stand on conservative principles. We speak to small and large private groups as well as churches.

Mr. Henderson shares the commission of the NC Faith and Freedom Coalition. I have set up meetings that allow Mr. Henderson to speak about the Woolworth sit-in and his passion for the civil rights movement. He enables me to give a brief commercial of our organization and fundraising during these meetings.

We were riding from one county to the next. I asked Mr. Henderson, "What were you going to order to eat if you would have been served at the sit-in." He responded, "No one has ever asked me that, and for a matter of fact, I did not even have money to pay for my lunch but had been promised by a friend that he would pay."

After hearing the response of Mr. Henderson, I was inspired to write this book. He is such a hero, and there are so many stories that he has to share and has shared that had never been recorded in a book form.

I encourage you to relax and travel back in time and glean from the stories of this living hero of history. You should also look into his current itinerary and meet us to hear how Mr. Henderson has progressed and his inspiration to help the next generation.

I have written five books for myself and three books for others, but this book ranks top on my list!

Dr. Paul Brintley, D. Min.
PO Box 551015
Gastonia, NC 28055
704.861.8555 office
DrPaul@PaulBrintley.com

SALUTING A HERO

By Jason Williams

In 2016, my wife and I, along with our five kids, took a trip to Washington, DC. It was the first time my children, Phillip, McKenzie, Meghan, Peyton, and Lucy, had been to the nation's capital. They were ages ten, nine, eight, six, and one. On that trip, we visited the Smithsonian Museum of American History.

As we made our way through the metal detector, there was an eye-catching exhibit to the right as soon as we entered. It was the counter from the infamous 1960 sit-in at Woolworth's restaurant. I told the kids how amazing it was to see something this historical knowing that it took place less than ninety minutes from our house. We marveled at the courage of these brave young men who dared to enter the restaurant. We were grateful for their boldness, which helped spark a movement that spread across the nation.

Little did I know that I would form a relationship with one of these historical figures less than two years later.

I met Clarence Henderson in 2018. I was honored to meet him and cherished every minute we conversed. I listened to him talk about how the civil rights movement had been hijacked by the left and how conservatism, entrepreneurship, and education choice was the remedy for the minority community.

Over the next couple of years, our relationship continued to grow. When we started the NC Faith and Freedom Coalition in 2019, it was only natural that he would be one of the first people I reached out to. He shared our vision of advancing conservative values and promoting a biblical worldview in our culture and government. He eagerly accepted the opportunity to join the organization as an ambassador.

When we brought Dr. Paul Brintley on the team, he began to travel with Clarence. He shared stories of their trips and the wisdom he gleaned from him. He approached me with the idea that we collaborate on this book. One of the reasons I was thrilled to assist was to chronicle Clarence's storied life and memorialize his contributions to the civil rights movement so that my kids and future generations will know his impact on our nation.

Helping with this project has been one of the most rewarding opportunities of my life.

FOREWORD

"If we open a quarrel between the past and the present, we shall find that we have lost the future."
Winston Churchill
June 18, 1940

IF EVER A group of Americans could open a quarrel with the past, it is Black people—carried to the land of opportunity and freedom in slave ships, stacked together like sardines. Millions of people from different nations in Western Africa, speaking other languages, were captured by slave traders or sold by rival Africans and forcibly taken to the western hemisphere. The brutality of the slave trade and the stench of disease was so intense, over two million died during the Middle Passage.

For nearly two hundred years, the descendants of these survivors served as chattel for Americans until the Civil War. Then to add insult to injury after being freed, these same men and women were forced to live under an unjust system of inequality where color determined rights for nearly another 100 years. The right to vote and where to eat and live were determined by race. A man's skin color regulated even public drinking water.

That was the world my friend Clarence Henderson was born into in 1941 in South Carolina. Yet, he not only helped to change that world during the 1960s, but he is helping to shape it today. When a photographer captured Clarence joined with three other young A&T students on the second day of a protest at the Woolworth lunch counter, they turned a simmering protest movement into a full-fledged fire that swept across America. Black people from Maryland to Kansas, New York to Texas, and beyond saw that photo and declared enough is enough.

Yet the true essence of Clarence was not just on display on February 2nd and throughout the spring protest movement in Greensboro, North Carolina. The essence of Clarence Henderson is wrapped up in his love for the American family and the American Republic. While some have settled for placing Americans in racial camps, where Blacks and other racial minorities are in the victim camp and Whites are invariably the oppressors, Clarence has opposed it. From Critical Race Theory to the Black Lives Matter movement, Clarence has supported one thing: a belief in the content of character, not the color of one's skin spoken of by Martin Luther King.

While the NAACP has decided that "reproductive rights" are now a civil rights issue, mainly because the organization's funding comes from liberal groups, Clarence has steadfastly supported the rights of the unborn and the destructive effects on our national soul when over sixty million children have been aborted, including nineteen million Black babies. On criminal justice reform issues, Clarence has championed for mainly minority defendants languishing in county jails in southeastern North Carolina without preliminary hearings. At the same time, the state Democratic Party and local Republican establishment continue to ignore their plight.

The American Constitution and the Declaration of Independence are Clarence's guideposts. When we fail to live up to the standards written by Madison and Jefferson, he will oppose those policies and practices. Yet, America will have no more outstanding champion to promote the words of the Declaration that all men are created equal and endowed by their Creator with certain unalienable rights, which include life, liberty, and the pursuit of happiness, than Clarence Henderson.

My friend wants a better America for his children, grandchildren and great grandchildren and yours and mine. It is simple faith in our Republic, and that greatness rests in America, and together, not apart, we will win the future. Enjoy this book, and I know I will as we learn what shaped an American icon and what is continuing to drive him today.

Rev. Kevrick McKain
Executive Vice President
Douglass Leadership Institute

Chapter 1

BIRTH AND CHILDHOOD

On September 18, 1941, I was born in Townville, South Carolina, what society would call *the wrong side of the tracks,"* except there were no tracks. Delivered by a midwife, I have no birth certificate. It was a farm, and our father was a sharecropper. What was unusual at that time was that my father and the sharecropper had become good friends. The sharecropper was a White guy, and my father named me after him. Being named after him helped set the tone for me to bridge the gap between the races.

When I was three or four years of age, I remember walking alongside my mother, trying to help her pick cotton in the cotton field. It was one of the fields where we picked cotton weekly. Most people think of hot days picking cotton, but those are not the only days of the year when cotton can be harvested. Cotton can also be picked early morning before sunrise and late in the evening when the sun has set. But rain or shine, the job still must be done. Thinking back on those early days all I can remember is picking cotton.

Javan and Hazel Henderson (Mother and Father)

It was time to move north, and my father decided that we all needed a change. Five areas will influence your belief system. These five areas will impact how you currently believe and what you expect from the future.

FIVE INFLUENCES OF YOUR BELIEF SYSTEM

1. Your environment
2. A credible authority's advice
3. Your personal experiences
4. The experiences of others
5. The Bible—the greatest to trump all others

My father knew that our environment in Townville would not yield the best harvest for his family. There were five of us: my mother, my father, and my two brothers; the oldest brother, Melvin, middle brother, Jvan; and me. And now I'm the only one left from that group. We came to Greensboro, North Carolina, in the late forties.

We ran out of gas on the way, and my father had to walk to the nearest gas station. I was sitting on my mother's lap and asked her why we had stopped. When she told me, I reached over and tried to start the car and received a slap on the hand for my effort. When we got to our destination, my father discovered that the movers following us had stolen his rifle.

We lived in a Black neighborhood. I attended an all-Black segregated school. I never went to an integrated school. It was all Black from grade one until high school graduation. I was within walking distance for the first two years in school.

When my dad came to Greensboro, he never worked for anybody but himself. I had a segregated education, but my father had a gift that God had given him. He knew auto mechanics up one side and down the other. If he heard a car running

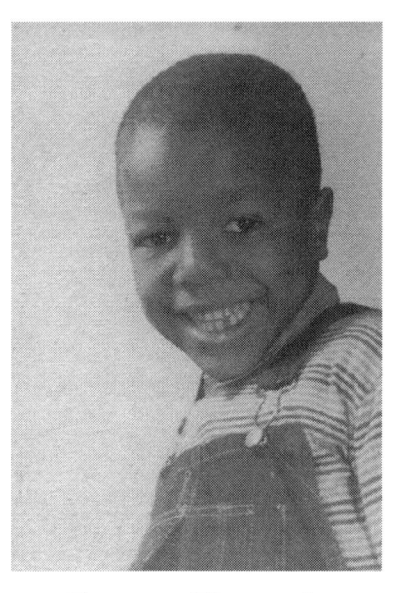

Clarence - First grade

and making an odd sound, he could tell you what was wrong with it without lifting the hood. I can remember car dealers bringing their vehicles to him from all over town. Their guys had a piece of paper on the wall certifying them, but they would get stumped on service issues they couldn't diagnose. My father could. My father would.

Clarence with Father, Javan

FORGOTTEN COURAGE

I remember everybody who lived in the neighborhood in Greensboro. We had doctors, lawyers, and sanitation workers living on the same street in that neighborhood. People from all walks of life lived there.

What happened with a new kid on the block, especially a young man? We were challenged every day. I had to fight every day to keep from getting beat up. And so that prepared me physically. I believe that makes my spirit as strong as it is right now. I continue to fight, but from a different point of view.

After those two years, my father moved us all into what you would call, believe it or not, as this was back in 1948 or 1949, an integrated neighborhood. There was a dusty dirt road that we drove onto that integrated neighborhood to the back and into the cul-de-sac. There were only four houses back there where Black people lived. But we were surrounded by White neighbors.

BLACK AND WHITE

ALTHOUGH WE LIVED among White neighbors, I was bussed to the all-Black schools. I rode the bus out of my neighborhood and passed several segregated White schools. And so, it allowed me to see things I would not have seen. It gave me firsthand experiences that are only mentioned in history books today. I lived it.

During lunchtime and breaks at school, I would play with the Black kids in my class. When I got home from school, there was only one Black kid my age. He and I played together daily. As we were playing, we heard some other kids coming our way. They were White, and we just ignored them. Our routine continued until one day we invited those White kids to play with us, and from that day forward, we played together, and ethnicity was never an issue among us. We had a huge yard, and it became a haven for all kids to play.

It was nothing for the White kids from the front of the neighborhood to come to the back and play all kinds of sporting games. We played without arguments about our color. That's when I understood that people are not born racist. Their parents didn't know where they were. Only when a few parents realized that their children were playing with Black kids did they explain that it was either forbidden or there should be separation.

One of my childhood memories is of Jvan and me going with my father to a friend's house who was White, and watching the fight between Joe Louis and Rocky Marciano. We didn't have a TV. My father would pull for Joe Louis, and his friend would pull for Rocky Marciano.

It was unusual for me to think of integration, although it was constantly around me. Although I experienced instances of racial bias, by no means would I let them define me.

When I was growing up, my oldest brother, Melvin, started paying whatever bills we had under the direction of my mother, because she did not like to go out much. As time went on, and my brother left home, that responsibility was passed to my middle brother, Jvan.

One evening, I remember my mother telling me that I would be going to town the following day to pay bills. I had watched my brothers do it and wondered if that would become my responsibility. My mother was a homebody. I learned to do all the transactions. At a young age, I learned to handle other people's money. I also paid various bills for my father because my father worked six days a week and went to church on Sunday.

Something usual that has become unusual is that I was born and raised in a household with a father and mother. I never heard my father curse or saw him smoke. He never said a bad thing about any White person whatsoever. He was so busy making a living for his family that he did not waste his time gossiping or running down anyone. My father took care of his family, even cutting my hair until I was paying for it myself. This was my father's pattern with my two brothers also. He was a self-made man.

TWO WATER FOUNTAINS

AS A YOUNG kid, I can remember going downtown with my mother to Woolworth's. Downstairs there were two water fountains, one for "Colored" and one for "Whites." I looked at those water fountains, and I saw the same water coming out and wondered what the difference was. Now, keep in mind that this was a public facility. And everything was the same upstairs, except for the lunch counter. At the lunch counter, we could purchase food, but we had to buy it to go. And so it was not unusual for my family to shop at Woolworth's. I went through that store for several years.

The F.W. Woolworth Co. had the first five-and-dime stores, which sold discounted general merchandise and fixed price, usually five or ten cents, undercutting the prices of other local merchants. As the stores popularly became known, Woolworth was one of the first American retailers to put merchandise out for the shopping public to handle and select without the assistance of a sales clerk. Earlier retailers had kept all merchandise behind a counter, and customers presented the clerk with a list of items they wished to buy (F. W. Woolworth Company - Wikipedia).

Little did I know that history would be made at that lunch counter as a kid.

Many shopping experiences influenced my belief system. My mother had a relative who lived in Pennsylvania. And I can remember like it was yesterday; my mother and father and I traveling to Philadelphia, Pennsylvania. We passed a White Castle restaurant. And my dad said, "I'm gonna stop and get us something to eat." Well, he stopped, and when he got out of the car, the sign on the door said open. We could see the clerk walk up and flip the available sign to a closed sign right as my father walked to the door. They even went so far as to close the blinds so he couldn't come into the restaurant. So, those are the kinds of things that were happening.

Around the age of nine, I remember riding my bicycle on the sidewalk. As a White man approached, I moved the bike out of his path. He, however, never once looked at me and stepped over and pushed me off the bike with his shoulder and kept walking. I was shocked that a grown man would go out of his way to do this.

It was nothing for me to be walking down the street and be called the N-word. That was nothing unusual. It would mostly be kids hanging out and walking up and down the street calling names. One time at my first job, I was called out of my name by a shopper.

As a teenager, I wondered what it would be like to have my own money. I quit the football team to go to work for a grocery store, bagging groceries. I would get out of school on Friday and work Friday evening and then all day Saturday for five dollars. Although that was a lot of hours, I had money in my pocket.

Many of these life experiences shaped my relationship with people. The things that I endured growing up have helped me build bridges for relationships. Standing and bagging groceries, I listened to thousands of conversations between families, friends, and foes. Take notes when you are around others. Listen to the way they describe what they are dealing with that day. The more you observe, the more you learn. Be aware of how people talk about things today, and do not be shocked to see how they may change tomorrow. Change is a good thing. People need room to change. We all need the freedom to be enlightened.

An excellent outlet for me was sports. Being part of a team is where I learned to work with others. I learned to compete and understand the game played on the court or the field. Your actions judge the game of life. Your life should not be impacted by what people say about you, but by how you play the game of life. Words can hurt, but you have to know deep inside who you are and how talented you are. Playing sports changed my life immensely.

SPORTS

I attended Dudley High School because it was the only Black school in our community. During those days, the White schools would not play sports against the Black schools. We could play as well as they could, and a lot of times better, but we were not allowed to compete against them. Those life lessons of knowing that we were just as good, if not better, shaped me and gave me a sense of resiliency that I carry with me even up to now.

I played three main games: baseball, football, and basketball. When I first learned how to play basketball, I built my own goal with a wooden backboard, found myself a big, long stick, and hung it up in the backyard. I used to be out there playing all the time. And I was pretty good at sports.

My best talent was football. I never played as a high school student because when I tried out for the team a job became available. So I quit playing football to work. I did play city league baseball and football, in which one side of town competed against the other side. I played those three sports as often as possible.

My position in basketball was a guard. Being a guard gave me the opportunity to lead the team. I could direct others as well as get myself involved in the plays. I was the coach on the court. We all need to touch the ball to feel that we are part of the team, and any good guard knows the importance of getting others involved.

As a football player, I shined as a running back. Running backs learn to lead from the second man position. The quarterback is the leader on the offensive side of the ball. He is the coach on the field and makes every effort to give the running backs and receivers all a chance to have the ball in their hands. I realized as a running back that I may not always get the ball and sometimes I would be a decoy for others to get attention. How well does that play in your life today when getting others involved?

Baseball is considered to be America's pastime, and I enjoyed playing first base for my team. Besides the pitcher and catcher, the first baseman gets more camera time action than any other player on the roster. He must be quick and aware of every hit, because the throw will be coming his way from the infield.

My baseball teams always competed for championships because of hard work and dedication. We went for the City League Championship and lost against one team from the other side of town.

My basketball career had its ups and downs. We, too, played for championships. In eleventh grade, I left high school to work, which hindered my career. I graduated from Brown Summit, where I was the star of that team. And we lost the first game of the season, but never looked back as we ended up playing in the championship. We had a pretty good year.

My defense was what propelled me to be a star. As a basketball guard, I learned to watch the guard and find his skill set and what he liked to do. With many studies, I could take the ball away from anyone. They may beat me another way, which was fine, but they wouldn't beat me doing what the guard liked to do.

That's when I learned how to put pressure on the ball. Pressure is a fantastic thing. It can cause people to do many things that they don't intend to do. Much like what happened with the civil rights movement, we put pressure on those who opposed us until they couldn't resist giving us our rights as American citizens.

CHILDHOOD CHALLENGES

INITIALLY, I WAS treated differently in school because my parents were not what you would call educated. And here's what it did. It made me that much stronger. I learned from my teachers in class, I was pretty good at reading books, and I didn't have any problems passing tests.

Once when I was in seventh grade, the teacher called on two of my friends. She said, "This person is a B student and this person is a B student, but Clarence is a C student." I made the same grades as they did! Those things made me understand that humanity is what it is, and people may say some things about you that are not true. Do not let those types of statements define you.

It's not necessarily about Black or White. It's about people's dispositions. I continued with that mindset until segregation ended. I started going to high school with the perspective that everyone mattered. We moved back to the other side of town, but I still had to catch the city bus to get to school or I would walk. It would take me thirty minutes each way. My parents didn't have the money for me to catch the city bus. The finances were not there to have all the luxuries many people had in those days.

Christmas at my house was below average. I can remember other kids getting presents at Christmastime, but what we got were clothes. So, as far as getting toys and those kinds of things, I never had them at my house because my father was the primary breadwinner.

My mother didn't go to work until after I started school, and that was a part-time job. But again, my dad, being the kind of guy he was, never drove a car. He had a car when we came from South Carolina. He always had a truck and used it to make money. He sold cardboard; he would go around town to the dumpsters, pick up cardboard, and load it on his truck. Another small income stream was selling bottles. He always knew how to turn a dollar, and occasionally he would extract copper and make money out of that.

He was a mechanic, but none of his sons knew anything about mechanics because all we saw was the dirt on his fingernails. I didn't understand him. He was a self-employed guy, a self-made person. People consistently asked for him to repair their vehicles. Even when he got to the point where he retired and couldn't do it anymore because he got sick, people would come by the house and want him to fix their car. He said many times, "I can't." They would say, "Well, can you at least come out and listen to it and see what's wrong with it." During those days, I didn't realize how smart my daddy was. Much later in life, I began to look at him differently because I thought I knew more than he did, especially after getting my college degree. But I found out he had all kinds of wisdom.

When my daddy first came to Greensboro, his idea was to buy a lot of property. And during that time, if you were married and wanted to purchase land, your spouse had to sign off. My mother was afraid that we would lose something. So, the only thing she would sign off on was for my dad to purchase his first house. Later he bought his second house, and she signed off on that, but when he started talking about buying property, she always backed out of those plans. A lot only cost $600 in those days, and my dad knew the future values would increase.

My grandfather on my father's side of the family was an entrepreneur. He had thirteen children, including my dad. They had a farm for many years before losing it to taxes. I heard some stories that it was not taxed, but it had been stolen from the family because it was prosperous. He was strictly a businessman, and in the summertime, my dad and his brothers would go to Florida and pick crops. They would take my dad for a few reasons, even though he was one of the younger brothers. They drove to Florida, and because my dad was a mechanic, he could repair the car if something happened to it during the journey.

My brothers and I were known as the three amigos. We stuck together. We had faith in each other because we had each other's back. When we first moved to Greensboro, we lived in a see-through house. You could see straight through these houses from the front to the back. Ours was a house that had been broken down into two apartments. We had an outside toilet. We were fortunate to have running water. Our clothes were cleaned and scrubbed by hand in the washtub. We only had cold water in the house. When we needed warm water, it was heated with wood. As far as living conditions, I've seen it all.

Brothers Jvan and Melvin with Clarence

CHILDHOOD CHALLENGES

The most challenging thing that I went through was acceptance. We were not what some would call today bourgeoisie Black folks. People would notice when we first moved to Greensboro that we were poor. We lived in the worst part of Greensboro at that time. We lived in the lower end, the worst part of that neighborhood. A place they called Dingham.

I encouraged myself to do better and that it was possible in America. It's not easy to muster up any vision when the living conditions are so poor, but I am proof that it can be done. I just learned that it had to be up to me if it was to be. And as a matter of fact, what helped me most was when I was in high school and my brother Jvan and I were pretty much the same size. I was able to wear his clothes. If not, I would have worn the same thing every day. I did not look at hand-me-downs as a negative. I appreciated my parents doing all that they could afford to do.

A great thing about my mother was that she was a phenomenal cook, and she'd make do out of just about anything. Those efforts drive me to make the best out of any situation.

At one point, I was very sick as a child; I had an infection in my ear. The doctor, at that time, used to make house calls and gave me some shots in my behind. I had to sit on my pillow for days from the pain. For some reason that doctor became very fond of me. He mentioned to my mother that he would like to adopt me. This doctor was a White man. He said he would like me to be his chauffeur when I grew up. My mother replied with an emphatic "No way." She said, "I'm not signing up for that!"

Like we see now, there was a danger of being put in a box by the other race. In many ways Black folks have always been put in containment. Human nature will always keep another man or class down under their power if allowed.

Going outside that neighborhood, beyond the imaginary boundaries, could get you locked up. Today some of us are living on reservations similar to the American Indians.

Those Black reservations have names like projects, ghettos, and lower-income housing in the heart of major cities like Chicago, Detroit, New York, and most urban areas. And we fail to understand that if we do not wake up to the hidden agendas, we could be stuck on the reservation.

I hear people all the time now talking about how we are victims or survivors. But we're not victims or survivors. We are overcomers. We are a strong race, but we don't realize that. I have observed that people have always tried to tell the Black race what they're supposed to do.

When Dr. Martin Luther King rose and began to lead us, it woke up America. We realized that we do not have to be told what direction to take. It was clear that we could think for ourselves. Too many people outside of our neighborhood were trying to tell us how to live and improve, yet they never lived under our conditions. If they don't live in the community, they have no idea what's required to fix that neighborhood. They say, "Well, you should do this, you should do that."

Our rent on Marsh Street was not much at all. I don't know what the cost of rent was at the Marsh Street address since I was so young. But on Oakland Avenue, a lady charged us five dollars a week. She would come down so far, sit in her car on Saturday evening, and when we saw her out there, we would meet her and pay her five dollars.

INJUSTICES

WHEN I WAS growing up, a Black man who lived in our community was accused of raping and killing a White woman. The neighbor was found guilty, and the only evidence presented was that the husband said he did it. He was convicted and put to death. It was not until the husband was on his deathbed and must have fallen under conviction that he confessed that he had raped his wife and lied about it to protect himself. The sad news is that the Black guy, falsely accused, lost his life by the death penalty.

When we lived on Oakland Avenue, we didn't have a TV. My mother used to let me go across the street because the family across the street had a TV. And as a matter of fact, the first time I read a *Jet* magazine was at their home. I can remember looking at that magazine and seeing Emmett Till—photos of his brutally murdered body before and after. It must have been about 8:00 at night when I went home, and I had to walk, not even a third of a block. I was apprehensive about going home because I was sure that some White person would jump out and do the same thing to me that they did to him. I could go on with the story after story of the fears that I lived through of racist situations we dealt with during that time.

The Alcoholic Beverage Control (ABC) law enforcement agency investigated criminal violations in the past. I remember one incident when they stopped my two brothers. Melvin had just bought a car, and Jvan was driving. They were arrested, and Jvan's jaw was broken during the stop. The reason for the stop was never determined. A lawsuit was filed, but the case was thrown out. Later, when Melvin became a police officer, he looked for the case file and couldn't find it. America then vs. America now.

We did have systemic racism during that time. We had a system of racism that enslaved people, because that's what slavery was and what Jim Crow was. But again, we need to understand that nobody can hold us down at this time. Only we can hold us down. I have realized that the way we were brought over to this country has been detrimental to us. We were brought over here to work the land. They divided us between the house and the field, and still today we have some of that.

One of the house-enslaved person's responsibilities was to report on the field-enslaved people. They knew their role pertained to the house and ensured that they could stay in that position. There is a mindset to ask others how we are doing as a people, almost to being colonialized to feel as if we always need outside approval. We think that others know better than we do, always asking them how well we are doing. White people have always understood who we are because we have great talent and skills. We were the ones taking care of their children, managing their businesses…the whole nine yards. And so, it is time for us to wake up and understand what happened. The movement consisted of two parts.

The first part—civil rights—was successful, but the second part —economic empowerment—was not put into place. We opened the door, then walked away and left everything on the table. So now, the new civil rights movement is economic empowerment.

INJUSTICES

We understand that money is a universal language, and that language speaks for itself. It was a financial impact on Woolworth's chain store that brought about the integration of that counter.

We have to take an honest look at this country called America and see that America now is not the America it was. We are not perfect, but when I keep hearing it said that we're the most racist country, that's certainly not so. One of its best proofs is that you have so many people who continue to come to this country. People travel here by foot, not knowing if they will live to taste freedom. They have heard and read about how great this country is. This country is offering them an opportunity for a better life.

So the other side of the story needs to be told, and we keep allowing people to rewrite history. For example, I never really thought about removing the Confederate statues because they are part of history. Now people want to tear them down. If you don't have that as a part of your history, you're doomed to repeat it. And so, it's been a great lesson for me to know that I can leave for my children, my grandchildren, and my great-grandchildren, a better America than I was born and raised and live in today. I turned eighty years old on September 18, 2021.

And so when I hear people right now talking about racism, most have no idea what racism is. It teaches you many things when you're called everything except by your name. I learned to mentally paint people in a corner where they couldn't get out. That was my way of speaking out to a person and making them admit something one way or the other.

RELATIONSHIPS THAT DEFINED ME

SOME OF MY teachers took extra time to ensure that their students learned at a high level. It happened with segregated schools, which was good; our teachers taught us precisely what we had to expect. And the teachers, for the most part, were very, very supportive of the kids and taught them what was required. I received an excellent education, the whole nine yards of learning.

All the coaches I've ever had were a great inspiration. However, if you want to look at who truly inspired me, look at my two older brothers. My oldest brother was drafted into the military and was sent to boot camp. They took him to Fort Jackson, South Carolina, and to California. It was not long until he was taken to Korea, where he almost got killed. In Korea, he was hit with a hand grenade and shot, and the bullet went straight through him. But he still, after that, came back and became a public servant, a police officer for seventeen years with the Greensboro Police Department.

One of my greatest blessings was being raised in a two-parent household. And my father wound up being my hero. If there were any other heroes for me, those people probably played sports. People like Jackie Robinson because I used to listen to him play baseball on the radio before we had a TV. Other athletes such as Jim Brown could give their all in every competition. And even to Jesse Owens—many people don't know how he helped destroy the idea about the master race when he went out and won all those Olympic titles in Germany. These are heroes who guided my thinking early in life.

My other brother, Jvan, affected my life too because we were four years apart. Once, our mother sent us out to the store on the corner, not too far from home. One afternoon, as we made our routine walk to the store, we noticed three Black kids. They got my brother and they had him swinging in the air. Some way fighting and tugging, but he got away from them and then ran them off; we went into the store and got the food for my mother. So, this taught me a great lesson, which is that freedom is not free. You always have to defend your freedom.

At the store that day, it dawned on me that somebody wanted to get something for nothing. My brother understood that our father had worked for that money, and these three kids decided they wanted to take the money they hadn't worked for. Those thieves felt as if they had some entitlement to our money. Today there is a false ideology of self-entitlement to something you believe you deserved when no efforts paid for it. They thought they were entitled to take my brother's money and do what they wanted. My middle brother and I were so close, and I never saw him afraid of anything. I mean, he would stand up to challenges from older kids. If he couldn't do anything else, he'd run away throwing rocks at them. I never saw him show fear.

My oldest brother stayed in North Carolina all his life except when he served in the military. But my middle brother left Greensboro when he was in eleventh grade. He got my father to sign off, and he went into the Navy for four years. Upon his return, he told me some stories about what he saw. He gave me comparisons of traveling overseas, and he constantly reminded me about how great America was, even though it was full of racism.

He talked about how he had seen a guy walking down the street with his hand cut off because he stole something, or had his foot cut off because he stole something. So he realized then that even though he was under those conditions, as an American, here, he has liberty. He moved from Greensboro to Washington, DC, and stayed there. And then, finally came back here. We were close. When you saw one, you always saw the other one.

My oldest brother and I were eleven years apart. There were two children born in my family who I never met because they died before I was born. Sickness and disease ran rampant in the Black community in those days, and many families lost babies due to the lack of health care. I think about those two being alive today if they had found a doctor's care, and now they would be adults. One of my brothers went blind. There was my sister who caught a fever, and she died. My parents had five kids, but the two kids between my middle brother and me died very young.

HIGH SCHOOL LIFE

I WENT TO Dudley High School. I don't think all the things that happened to me would have happened except that God was on my side. When I was in eleventh grade, we had a concert at A&T. I had played saxophone from the seventh grade through to my freshman year at A&T. It was hard to believe that one day that I would march in the band at a university that I dreamed of attending. It was still a college in those days.

All my dreams changed instantly as an altercation at A&T broke out, and I was involved. There were nine of us who were expelled. Three of us were from the Southside at the time, and everybody else came back to campus before we did. My father brought us to school and went in and talked to the principal about allowing us back into the school. The principal agreed to let my best friend and me back in, but a stipulation was attached. He said, "I'm going to let you guys back in, but you will have to repeat your grade." What a blow below the belt! And I hadn't flunked anything.

My father's reaction was to get up and walk out of the office. I did not know what he was thinking or where he was going. After my father left, my best friend and I were told to go to class, but we left the campus, and he flagged down a passerby, and we caught a ride to Brown Summit High. We went in, and we were enrolled. That's how I went to Brown Summit High School.

I had never thought about going to college. But when I went out to Brown Summit, my friend and I took a test, and we scored the highest score in the school. Until then, we didn't appreciate the level of training that we had at Dudley. It was not smart to get expelled from such an incredible high school. I got expelled from Dudley in the eleventh grade then enrolled into Brown Summit High School, where I graduated.

Clarence – Brown Summit High School Graduate 1959

I did not think anything about it, but A&T sent the enrollment application a short time later. This was the predestined path that led me to A&T. I didn't have it in my mind to attend college. I'm the only person out of my immediate family who graduated college. So I didn't have any references. My goal was to finish high school. But I never thought of myself as college material. God had a different design in mind for me. And it changed my life because if I had stayed at Dudley and graduated, I probably would never have gone to A&T and never would have been a part of the sit-in.

Brown Summit didn't have a band. I had been a part of a band back at J.C. Price Middle School. I started in the seventh grade, and I played in the marching band at Dudley High School. During my first year at A&T, I played in the marching band there. I was first sold on the marching band of A&T as a kid. They were the highlight during our Christmas parades. The uniforms, sound, and swagger caught my eyes, and I always wanted to be in that band.

HIGH SCHOOL LIFE

FIRST YEAR OF COLLEGE

I WENT TO college, and I lived off campus because my parents couldn't afford a dorm, so I didn't know about the sit-in until the second day. One guy by the name of Ezell Blair told me about it. He and I started in the first grade and went to A&T together. He came to the downstairs student lounge at A&T, and he began to tell me about what they had done the first day at Woolworth's. Then he asked, "Would you want to participate?" That simple question is how I got involved.

College life was new to my family and me; I didn't know what to expect. I was not ready for college. I chose a major that I didn't even like. I majored in biology because one of my friends had chosen biology. And so, it got to the point that I would go to class sometimes, and sometimes I wouldn't. And that's why Ezell found me in the lounge that day before the sit-in on the second day. I was sitting in the Bluford Library downstairs in the lounge then. I was supposed to be in class.

When Ezell approached me, he began to tell me about the day before. It was interesting to hear that they had been a part of a sit-in. I left A&T with him that day, February the second. We walked down to F.W. Woolworth and walked in that door. That day was different than any other time of my life. Frankly, I didn't know how I would come out at the end of the day—in a vertical position, handcuffed, going to jail, or in a horizontal position on a gurney being sent to the hospital, even the morgue. The entire perspective of that day changed my life forever.

I am often asked if I was afraid to be at the sit-in that day. I tell them how rough my neighborhood was, but it never gave me the fear of being at the sit-in. The police came in during that day, looked at us, and walked out because those guys, on the first day, had taken them by surprise.

I had no money to buy food, and I asked Ezell, "What will we do if Woolworth's decides to serve us?" Ezell promised me that he would pay for whatever I ordered. He never had to pay a dime because I never ate at that lunch counter. I did it because it was something that needed to be done. Someone had to change the narrative. My determination stemmed from all that I had gone through growing up; when I had the opportunity to compete, rather than compare. I was eighteen years of age, and my parents found out about it because they saw the newspaper.

On the first day, Joseph McNeil, Franklin McCain, David Richmond, and Ezell Blair. Joseph McNeil, Franklin McCain, William Smith, and me on the second day. When the news began to spread, my name was not mentioned with the other three regarding the picture taken on the second day. Most of my family was upset about me not getting recognized, but that is not why I did it. I knew I was there. The history was soon corrected, and I have been known all over this country for that historic event.

During that time, there was a bomb threat against us. The Ku Klux Klan, aka the KKK, came in, but we did not leave. There were all kinds of things constantly being said to us by patrons of Woolworth's. We had been called many different types of names, but we still sat there.

We put Jim Crow on trial, and Jim Crow was found guilty. I learned from this demonstration about due process; that the American public has a right to assemble peaceably. Our main caveat was that, no matter what, we were going to remain peaceful.

The powers that be went to the president of A&T College to get us to change our minds. The mayor of Greensboro and others demanded that if we didn't stop the sit-in, we should be expelled from school. The president of A&T College wisely said we could remain students if we attended classes and did not cause any disturbance and that what we did on our own time was not the college's responsibility. It gave us fuel to get our message out.

Some White people did participate in the movement for a short time, but that's not written down in the history of the sit-in. Uniquely, others came to our aid as the likes of Ralph Johns, who was Syrian. He had a clothing store near A&T's campus. He sold men's clothing. And many guys would go in there and buy his clothes because he had clothes that had come from New York. He was the one who planted the seed for eleven years about the sit-in before it came to fruition. He said, "If you guys want to be heard, do something like a sit-in." I found out later about his inspiration for the movement. He had talked to several A&T students. No one caught the vision other than Joseph McNeil, who finally rallied the other three guys to do it. Joseph was from New York. He went home for winter break and he came back to A&T ready to make a change.

When Joseph arrived back at the Greensboro bus station at 2:00 a.m., he rushed to the dorm and began to plan the sit-in. He wanted to be confident they would serve him, thinking things may have improved. So he went back to campus, and he told his roommate and the other two. Joseph said, "Now it's time for us to go do it." And that's how it got started.

When they sat down at the counter on February first, the idea was that they would go back to campus the next day and start recruiting people to participate. That's how they got other people involved. Note that young people, not older people, start all movements. Most of our parents were concerned that they might lose their jobs. All kinds of things may happen. At one point, I saw as many as 500 people inside of Woolworth's with standing room only. Both sides of the streets were lined with people. On the side street where Woolworth's was, people followed along with us, and on the other side were people who were against what we were doing.

One thing that I will never forget is how much it set a fire in others to protest. There was an economic impact playing a part at Woolworth's and other retailers. Dr. Willa B. Player from Bennett College went across the street from Woolworth's to a department store and stated, "Until y'all start serving us across the street, then I won't buy anything else from you" as she cut up her credit card in front of the clerk. Those were the pressures put on the other retailers that caused people to change their minds and join us.

Several meetings were attempted to negotiate with us, but they would not concede to open the lunch counter. Many older people said it's just not our time, and we were rushing it. Meanwhile, Dr. King came to A&T, and he was going to speak there, but they didn't allow him to, so he went over to Bennett College and spoke over there.

Only three Black people worked at Woolworth's, and they were the three people who sat down and had the first meal there on July 27, 1960.

It started on February 1st, 1960 and lasted 176 days before it ended on July 27, 1960. When A&T closed for summer break, Dudley High School students continued the sit-in to integrate the lunch counter. You don't see that talked about in history, other than the movement.

The sit-in happened before I went to New York. I worked a couple of years and even did some janitorial service and other odd jobs to make ends meet. When I realized that I was going to New York, I decided I was never coming back to Greensboro except to visit my parents.

MILITARY SERVICE

I WAS A member of the ROTC my first year at A&T. The ROTC program put a foundation in my life for structure and discipline. I am grateful for the time I spent with my instructors and colleagues. After attending A&T that first year, I started working on getting money to go back for the second quarter, I met my first wife, and I immediately fell for her looks instead of anything else. And God bless my mother, she told me, "This is not the woman for you," but I didn't listen. "You're going in one direction, and she's going in another." But I understand now how hardheaded we can be at some points in time.

I decided I would leave Greensboro, North Carolina, and never come back again except to visit my parents. But never say never. I moved to New York City and managed a shoe store on 125th Street in Harlem, and I saw people like Sidney Poitier, Muhammad Ali, and James Brown. And suddenly, I got this culture shock. During that time, we had the draft, and one of the worst things we've done in this country is eliminating the draft—people who don't understand what it means to defend this country.

So, I got this call from my mother, and she said, "Uncle Sam sent you a letter, they want you." I said, "What did you tell him?" She said, "I don't know where he is." Well, you see, Uncle Sam has a way of finding you. I got that same letter on 117th Street in Harlem about six weeks from then. And I went to Brooklyn to see if I was fit for the military. There were three of us who were from Greensboro. I'm the only one they called. My first wife and I divorced before I entered the military. So picture this; they put me on a twin-engine plane, didn't ask if that was the way I wanted to travel, and sent me to Fort Jackson, South Carolina. From there, I was sent to Fort Gordon, Georgia, but Uncle Sam still wasn't through with me. He sent me to Fort Rucker, Alabama, where I spent sixteen months when George C. Wallace was governor.

When I was stationed in Fort Rucker, Alabama, a few of us decided to go to the Dothan club. The first city outside of the fort was Enterprise. On this evening, we had a flat tire, and while we were changing it, the sheriff came up and asked, "What are you boys doing? (as if it weren't obvious). Then he said, "You boys better have that tire changed before the sun goes down." I don't know what would have happened because we changed it before then.

When I completed my time in the service I said I would never be in George Wallace's country ever again. After getting out of the military, I met another young lady and proposed marriage, although my mother warned me again. But, you know, I was one of those guys who thought I could "fix it" during

Served in US Army 1966–1968

MILITARY SERVICE

that time, even though I saw the same things that my mother saw. I felt like I could fix her, so I married her. But it's a well-learned lesson that you can't heal anybody. It's up to them to make any changes. I didn't listen, and it cost me dearly. I was married for nineteen years, although we were separated for most of those years.

When I graduated from A&T, I got a job in Laurel, Maryland. I later found out that the apartment I rented was only a few blocks from where George Wallace was shot. How ironic was that?

N. C. A&T, State University Graduate 1972

BUSINESS ENGAGEMENT

AFTER EIGHTEEN MONTHS in Laurel, Maryland, I received a promotion but had to move to Columbus, Ohio. When I told Jvan where I was driving, he lived in Landover, Maryland. He told me that he had been stationed there and advised me not to take the job. I never associated that Columbus was near West Virginia.

Before moving, I was interviewed by the person who was to be my supervisor along with his supervisor. At the end of the interview, I was asked what I thought. But before I could answer, one of them said, "And we aren't prejudiced either." An alarm bell went off in my head, but I ignored it.

My job title was territorial manager, and the job provided a company car. The company policy called for the vehicles to be replaced after a number of miles. My car was exchanged for a new one. However, I was told that the company manager was taking my car and giving me his.

I remember another incident that happened when we had a company-client party. When my wife and I were introduced, the supervisor who called himself the "silver fox" said, "This is our newest employee, and his wife is pretty, but he sure is ugly." Then one of the clients said, "And he has big lips too."

I was assigned a specific number of clients in my territory, and on one occasion, I called one of them on the phone. He pretended that he thought I was my supervisor, and he proceeded to state that I was a smart aleck and I had made a pass at his wife. His wife looked around sixty-five years old and I was thirty-four. I told my supervisor what had happened, and his solution was to take that client from me. Shortly after that, I was terminated.

I was able to get an interview with the same company located in Chicago. After reviewing my performance when I worked in Laurel, they said I did an excellent job, but stated that they were told that my performance in Columbus was subpar. As a result, I was black-balled. Shortly after that, I moved my family back to Greensboro.

One of the jobs I took when I moved back to Greensboro was with a junior college. I started teaching business courses on a part-time basis. Later I changed to full time as a recruiter. After that, I was promoted to director of admissions. When the president of the college left, I applied for that position. I was told it required a PhD. After that, I was asked to train the new president, and later, when I informed the home office in Charlotte that he did not know what he was doing, their response was to terminate me. From there, I went into business for myself for almost thirty years.

A former football coach inspired me regarding the business types I have owned. The business's name was A.L. Williams, and then when he sold it, they changed it to Primerica. He sold it to Citigroup. Whenever Primerica became an entity, it was listed on Wall Street.

In addition to the civil rights movement, I was involved in what I would call a financial services movement. We exposed the insurance industry for what it was and exposed all the other sectors in the financial services to help the people in America understand how to purchase financial products. And not only that, but we also recruited people and trained them so they could become a part of our business. At one point, if you did the things that the company required, you could own your own company within Primerica. And they're still going strong now.

For example, there is a guy I worked with. When I met him, he was $300,000 in debt. When I left Primerica, he told me he was worth twelve million dollars.

It wasn't him. It was the system, and his following that system and submitting to that system shows you how America operates and how people in America operate. Primerica doesn't want to seek the highest prices for customers. They look for the best all-around product for the client and their family.

I traveled quite a bit with that guy. Our home office was in Georgia. And to show you how thrifty he was, we often would leave Greensboro with an almost empty gas tank and not fill up until we got to South Carolina because the prices were lower. These are significant lessons that I have learned and continue to learn because I'm very conscious of expenses. I always look for a deal because now and then, you get it.

During my tenure at Primerica Financial Services, Inc., I was a regional vice president and the audit and compliance officer for other regional vice presidents' offices within our organization.

But that business taught me about America's free-market capitalistic system, which most people don't understand. They don't understand that the system doesn't care who owns it. One of the most outstanding examples of that would be McDonald's. How can a seventeen-year-old kid working in McDonald's make a burger just like a forty-year-old can? Well, McDonald's has a system. Ray Kroc put a plan in place, and that system runs the business, and the people who work there work that system. It's simply placing that hamburger on a grill and cooking it in one minute and twenty seconds. And when a line gets three deep, they open another line until they have all lines open. For years, most fast-food chains only had one register, but McDonald's set a standard for multiple lines.

The McDonald brothers brought an idea of one restaurant, and people stood in line, but Ray Kroc saw McDonald's worldwide. And so, in simplistic language, a person who goes into business for themselves has a chance to do very well. But if you have a distribution system, you can become very wealthy because you can work forty hours a day by having forty people work for you one hour a day. When you understand how to leverage that team system, it changes your perspective on making money. And that's why I'm so adamant about the most extensive welfare system in America—our government—because they don't produce anything. Still, they live off the backs of the people in the private industries and want to take more and more money from them through taxes and other things.

Primerica - Top Regional Leaders Award

OTHER OPPORTUNITIES

On various occasions, especially in February, people would call me to come and speak about the Woolworth sit-in, and I decided I would organize a business out of it. I started doing speeches, and people would call, and I would not charge a fee. But at some point, I decided that I would charge a fee. The Bible says, "A laborer is worthy of hire." I have made a business out of it and have done well. When one door closed, God opened another door.

Chapter 2

FAMILY

BEFORE MY THIRD marriage, I told God that this is one of my weaknesses: I make the wrong choices. I had been adamant with my two brothers that I was never getting married again. But lo and behold, I was invited to speak at a prayer breakfast at my oldest daughter's church. Theresa had asked me to come over, and she said, "I also have a woman that I want to introduce you to." I don't know why she thought she could pick a woman for me. I got there, and Robin immediately caught my attention, although she was not the lady my daughter had in mind for me to meet.

Robin was helping in the preparation and serving the breakfast that day. As I went down the buffet line, my approach was "What school do you attend?" And Robin said, "Bless your heart." because she was thirty-nine. She tells people that was my pickup line. That was the start of our relationship on February 12, 2000. And we talked just about every day from that day until December 31, 2000, when we got married. She was, and is, a Proverbs 31 woman. Robin is from Conover, North Carolina.

Clarence and Robin's wedding December 31, 2000

She prepared all the food for our wedding, which shows you how dynamic she is. It is excellent how God introduced me to the right woman. The past twenty-one years have been great for both of us, and we have made great strides together.

First and foremost, she was a Christian lady, and we had a lot of the same goals. We were both in business for ourselves, headed in the same direction.

I have two biological children, Theresa, who lives in Walkertown, North Carolina, and Hazel, outside Atlanta, Georgia. With the help of my parents, I raised two children as a single parent. Currently, I have been blessed with a total of six grandchildren and nine great grandchildren.

Clarence with daughters Hazel and Theresa

I have two stepdaughters, Lisa and Tonia, who have been integral parts of my life. Since they were little kids growing up, they have always called me Daddy.

The girls have influenced me from the standpoint of learning that God knew what he was doing when he said male and female parents

FAMILY 41

would be there to guide them home. And they would be married before they started having any children.

I thought I could be both a father and mother to my two biological daughters, but I found out differently. One day, when conversing with my mother, she told me things that my daughters were telling her that were not revealed to me. It made me aware that there were things that children growing up may feel more comfortable talking to the mother or the father depending on the child's gender, based on whether the child is a male or female, and desire to speak to the same sex about life issues. But all these are life-learning lessons for me, and again, I share them as the opportunity arises.

My father had his first house built. And right next door was this family and this woman who had several children. Her oldest child came to live with her and brought his girlfriend with him, and they had six children. He wound up leaving Greensboro and going to New York and left his girlfriend and kids there with his mother for her to take care of. I made a vow to myself at that point in time that if I ever impregnate a woman, I will take care of that child. That vow has stuck with me because it happened with my second daughter, where I put off getting a divorce for many years.

Imagine having a daughter, my oldest daughter, and being in school, with a course load of twenty-one hours, and then working a full-time job, eight to ten hours a night. It gave me a new outlook on parenting. I am delighted that I went through those experiences. It was a life lesson, and I share those experiences with people when it comes up. I can tell people what a good marriage is and what a bad marriage is.

My wife, Robin, was in business before she met me. She graduated from Winston-Salem State University (WSSU). After working there for fifteen years, she decided to go into business. She had always baked and put together parties during her college years and working at WSSU. So, she opened up her own catering business. She eventually closed that business and started consulting and contracting with small companies offering start-up services, administrative support, and payroll services. She ended up with one client who wanted her to work with him exclusively. This decision did not come easily, since she transitioned to become self-employed; however, after some consideration, she did take the offer as operations manager. Two months after our marriage, the business was moved to Georgia, and Robin was making that commute. She would come home on Thursday or Friday. We lived in Greensboro at that time, and then she would go back to Atlanta on Sunday.

She was on her way to Atlanta when 9/11 occurred. Being alone and driving into that city while listening to the mayhem unfolding that day was incredibly traumatizing, not knowing where they may strike next. Because of the stress, she was unable to work that week due to a severe attack of vertigo. At that point, she decided that she needed to be here in Greensboro. So, she completed that year in Atlanta, and we restructured my business. She would work on handling all the paperwork in that business as an administrative assistant, which offered financial services such as life insurance, investments, mortgages, and long-term care insurance.

We started working together in 2002. We did that until I closed the business in 2010. But what that business did was teach me about America's free-market, capitalistic system, which most people don't understand.

My two brothers and I had an office together, and my oldest brother first retired, and then my middle brother. I stayed in the office for a while, finally closing it down. It proved that God has a plan for you that's better than your plan.

CHRISTIAN FAITH

BACK IN MY twenties, when I first heard about knowing Jesus, I was working at this place where they made bricks, and they had what we called Jesus freaks back then. I laughed at them when they approached me and wanted to talk to me about Jesus. But God still had a plan for me at forty-nine years of age. I met this gentleman while I was in business for myself, and one of the things we did was recruit people. I saw this guy talk to people. He had the suit on and looked like a sharp guy. I approached him about the business, and he told me, "I am on another journey, but let me pray for you and your business." At this point, I'm not born again, and my stomach is saying, "You don't need him to pray for you." But thank goodness I didn't tell him that I didn't want him to pray for me, so he did. We went on, and I saw him again, at the same shopping center, and he prayed for me the second time.

My brother Jvan's first wife had died, and I went to his house. Reverend James Smith was the man who had prayed for me, and there he sat with his wife. I don't know how he and my brother met, but Reverend Smith had started a Bible study class at his house. My oldest brother, Melvin, and Jvan began to go to his Bible studies.

My brothers and I would sit in the office and talk about the Bible while we operated an office together, and I decided to go with them to Bible study. I said to myself, *I'm going to go this evening.* I think it was on Tuesday. They were sitting in the back conference room, about to head out for the day, and we met in the hallway. I let them know that I was going with them to the Bible study, and they said, "Well, we were just going to invite you."

That evening, I went to Reverend Smith's house, and he led me to the Lord! Even when I didn't know who God was, I knew I was not born again.

It showed me that people who are not Christians have a veil over their hearts. If they would be open enough to listen and say, "Well, I've tried everything else. Why not try this?" God is sitting there waiting for us to receive the invitation he continues to extend to us.

I have only been a member of two churches in my life. First, at Shiloh Baptist Church, I started attending the Cathedral of His Glory. When I started going there, I was not born again. I knew I needed to change churches because I was teaching a Sunday school class for men at the Shiloh Baptist Church, and I was not even born again. At that time, I didn't know what that was, and they did not emphasize it.

I'm still a member of the Cathedral of His Glory. I'm the head elder there. It is a nondenominational, integrated church where all races attend. One of the funny things about it is that a friend who I grew up with asked, "Could you not find a Black pastor?" But I was looking for the Lord and not a pastor.

When you share things with me, I will not believe you if you don't have something to back it up and I see proof that it is true. If there is no proof, it is an opinion, and everybody has one. I was fortunate enough to join a church where the pastor was well versed in the Bible. When he shared things, he shared the history and how it came to be, so it fits in line with how I think. The pastor's name was Dr. C. Paul Willis. Oh, yeah, he was White. And there was a lot of controversy because he was the first pastor in Greensboro to invite Black members. Some of the

Black pastors became upset. But he said that God had told him that he would build an integrated church, which he did.

Dr. Martin Luther King Jr. said the most segregated time of the week is Sunday morning at eleven o'clock, and that should not be, and we shouldn't allow that to be so. It's unfortunate that within the church, you have a lot of pastors who put a lot of emphasis on the color of one's skin as opposed to the spiritual side of it.

When you're the leader of a flock, you have a great responsibility, and you have to look at what the Word of God says and not what you might think. To the church, we're in a position now to turn this whole world around. But we have to show ourselves approved and realize that it is our responsibility, because God says, "My people perish from the lack of knowledge."

Everybody is coming out of the closet, except Christians. A few years ago, when Hillary Clinton ran for president, the Douglass Leadership Institute distributed a book named *Protecting Your Ministry* written by Alliance Defending Freedom. Churches need to go back and review their bylaws and make sure that they cover what is allowed and what isn't allowed in church. Because if there is a gray area, the church can be exploited and sued if it is unclear what the church's bylaws and their rules and regulations are.

When my former pastor passed away, his son Dennis took over the role of senior pastor. Pastor Dennis Willis continues with the vision of building the Cathedral of His Glory.

I have worked as an usher, head usher, Sunday school teacher, finance committee member, coordinator of new members class, and now head elder. I will continue to work within the church, leading others to Christ for His Glory!

The youth pastor found out that I had participated in the civil rights movement, and he asked me to come speak with the youth group. I spoke at the youth meeting one evening. Pastor Dennis had all four of his children attending the youth group meetings. He said what caught his attention was when his children returned and spoke with him about what I had said in that meeting. They never talked about anybody who had come before with such excitement. He wanted to hear what I had to say, so he had me speak at one of our men's ministry meetings. Then, I spoke at two Sunday morning services after that.

One of the biggest things we need to recognize is that the changes will be made in America and worldwide through the church. But the church has to become prepared to pick up this movement and start to move like the Israelites moved. They didn't move unless they all moved. They crossed the land, going toward the Promised Land, and we have to become in one accord, because we're all here to build God's Kingdom. And it's not about Clarence Henderson. It's about what God wants and what He created us to be. We are put here for Him, and we have become vessels for Him to use us as He would. We become vessels when we get Jesus Christ, and we receive the Holy Spirit. We must have the trinity on the inside of us; through discipleship, the church can teach its members more and more about what it means to be a Christian.

THE HOLY SPIRIT

AFTER MY FIRST year at A&T, I lied about my age to work at this little nightclub. I will never forget one particular night when I had gone home twice that night, and my mother said, "You never come home while you are working, so maybe you need to stay." I ignored it. I went back, and I guess it wasn't fifteen minutes before someone had cut me from behind.

I have all these lessons to draw from, as to how things are revealed to us because I know you have heard it before, "My first mind told me." But that's the spirit telling you

Clarence with Dr. Paul Brintley, Ambassador at NC Faith and Freedom Coalition

and warning you about the direction you need to be going in at that moment.

So it's not just one specific thing, but a litany of things that have occurred in my life that I know the Holy Spirit was behind the scenes. I have learned to do introspection. When you look at yourself in the mirror, you don't see what you look like because it is outside, and God sees the inside. If you want to know who you are and what you look like, you ask Him. You may not like what He says, but at least it'll give you the direction that you need for your future.

I advise people to listen to that inner voice. If I do it my way, most of the time, I will end up in situations I shouldn't be in. But if I listen to the Holy Spirit, He will guide me. In those cases, what God has planned for me is better. His plan for me is better than my plan for myself.

Forty years passed before I was recognized for the sit-in, but I didn't complain. I think that the fact that I didn't murmur or complain set me up for today. God says, "Now I'll raise you because now I see that I can use you." People need to understand that God does not necessarily take an individual and put them in a position for that person, but for His people because that's what happened with Moses. It was not for Moses's benefit as it was for him leading people to the Promised Land.

HEALING THROUGH SCRIPTURES

Much can be said about good health care. Before 2010, I took no medication whatsoever. Then in 2010, on a regular visit to the VA to get a check-up on a hearing disability, my primary physician said, "You have blood in your urine. We need to check this out." The previous physician saw the same thing and told me it was not a problem. Fortunately for me, they caught it in time. I had a partial nephrectomy of the left kidney through a robotics procedure at Baptist Hospital in Winston-Salem. I had excellent care. Shortly after that, in 2013, I had another cancer attack, this time of the prostate. Again treatment was at Baptist Hospital, where I was given rounds of radiation to eradicate the tumor. I know the Veterans Administration gets a bad reputation; aside from the missed diagnosis, or should I say, no diagnosis of my previous doctor, I have had excellent health care and follow-up through the VA. I have been taught, and I have learned that God's word is alive. We can take what Jesus said, "If you say unto the mountain, 'Be thou removed and be cast into the depths of the sea,'" we can see, we can continue to say these things until they manifest themselves. I stand on that. See, some of the things people say are "I have cancer," "I have this," or "I have that." But I don't have it because it's not a part of my body. My body has been attacked by it. So, death and life are in the power of the tongue, and we need to speak life and not death.

Use the scriptures like medicine! Because doctors can only do so much, I realized the Holy Spirit could go where no doctor's hand could. It has helped me immensely to agree with what the Bible says. The Lord Jesus has changed my life tremendously. I see things happening in this world today, and I ask God to reveal to me what he's doing currently. What He's doing is exposing all the corruption and asking the Christians, "What are you going to do about it?" We're supposed to call all these things out and not be silent, because silence means consent. When we begin to call them out, it allows change because God, for the most part, announces it before He announces it. For example, he said to the two brothers, Cain and Abel, "Sin is at your door. And what are you going to do about it?" Cain ignored it and wound up killing his brother.

So, the most excellent and actual book there is, is the Bible. The Bible was given to us to provide and teach life. These other books may teach us how to earn a living, but as far as life is concerned, there's only one book: the Bible.

In July 2019, I was stricken with a severe attack of sciatica. I could not get out of bed for days. Through prayer and the assistance of physical therapists, chiropractors, and an acupuncturist, I have overcome. There is so much more for me to do, so I get it together with the Lord's guidance and keep it moving.

Then came COVID in August 2021. I had attended two homegoing services within days of one another. One night I got to the point where I couldn't breathe. My wife had to call 911, which helped me when they administered oxygen. They had to keep me on oxygen for seven days to assist my breathing. So, the challenge with

COVID for me are the mixed messages and lack of long-term research. One issue I am adamant about is that the choice should be left up to the individual as to whether they take the shot. I was hesitant to take the vaccine because of the partial removal of my left kidney a while back due to cancer, and then dealing with prostate cancer. I wanted to make sure that I wouldn't put something in my body that hurt me more than helped.

Each day, my wife and I would pray that our bodies would return to what they were before the COVID attacked us.

Healing scriptures are so important, and the Holy Spirit spoke to me. "You need to start reading healing scriptures." I ignored it. I think that was the hedge of protection that I needed. Because God, in His wisdom, knew some things that were going to attack me. I learned through this process that when you get that answer from the Holy Spirit, listen very carefully. Because, as I dealt with COVID, I was lying at night in my bed, and the Holy Spirit said to me, "You need to pay attention to what the Word of God says, his literal word, his written word, because he knows everything, and you just know some things."

It's like when you have a decree from heaven. It's been a great lesson for me when it's like what Joseph said to his brothers: "What you meant for harm, God changed for good." So this thing that was meant for harm has changed me for good. It's more apparent than I've seen before the church's role. That is, we need to understand the assignment that God has given us. The authority that we must carry out that assignment as the body of Christ, each has various talents that we can use to build His kingdom. Because He has chosen that we will be the ones to take back the earth and not God himself, and we will do it through His son, Jesus. Understanding that the ministry of God is in Christ and the ministry of the church is in Christ has changed things significantly for me.

COMMUNITY SERVICE

I HAVE BEEN involved in civic organizations, community initiatives, and volunteerism throughout my life. I've been on several committees. It is important to me to be involved in my community. That is part of being a citizen of the United States. Being a part of finding solutions for what might be affecting the community at large is always rewarding. In the past, I served as the chairman of the fundraising committee for the Gate City Chapter of the local chapter for North Carolina A&T State University. I also did the same thing for Bennett College. I was a board member for the Boy Scouts of America, Inc. in Greensboro. For several years, I served as secretary for the Dudley High School Hall of Fame, Hall of Distinction. The organization recognizes the achievements of its graduates and raises funds for scholarships for current graduates enrolling in college.

Also during this time, I was appointed to be the chairman of the Martin Luther King Jr. Commission of North Carolina. The main objective for the commission was to promote an awareness and appreciation of the life and philosophy of Dr. King, with a focus on reaching children under fourteen years of age. The commission engages youth within our regions with fellowship, panel discussions, and motivational speakers, and facilitate educational activities that enhance Dr. King's philosophy. Qualifying students receive awards and scholarships on behalf of the commission. During the month of January, the commission awards applicants with grants based on approved criteria and they participate in the State Employees MLK Jr. Observance and NC MLK Jr. Commissions Bell Ringing Ceremony.

2013 Swearing-in Ceremony for new North Carolina Martin Luther King Jr. Commissioners

BELL CEREMONY HONORS MARTIN LUTHER KING JR.

Clarence Henderson, chairman of the North Carolina Martin Luther King Jr. Commission, listens as Jacquie Jeffers reads a poem during a bell ringing ceremony observing King's birthday Friday at Bicentennial Plaza in Raleigh.

2016 NC Martin Luther King Jr. Commission Bell Ringing Ceremony in observance of Martin Luther King Jr. birthday.

I currently serve on the Phoenix Academy Charter School Board in High Point, North Carolina. I have people consistently wanting me to become a board member based on the information that I bring, and the knowledge and expertise I give to them. The only drawback is some boards have age limits and I am unable to serve. It's great to be able to be a good influence within your local community.

I am currently serving on the North Carolina General Assembly Statuary Hall Selection Committee, and as the North Carolina Chief Justice's Public Trust and Confidence Committee Chairman.

POLITICAL

After retiring from my business, I began to receive more requests for speaking engagements—namely at schools—sharing my experience in the sit-in. However, my engagement in the political arena became more prevalent. Around this time the climate of the country was dismal. People were concerned about the direction of the country and some simply had lost hope.

My speeches were intent on inspiring, motivating, and calming the fears. The only thing that conquers fear is faith. Faith that all will be well in the future. I encouraged them to get involved to help make that change.

I attended a GOP meeting in Greensboro in 2013 and told them, "You need me." I made that claim because the Democrats are great at setting the narrative—more often than not a false narrative. I saw that there was a lack of engagement with the Black community because they had given up on ever capturing the Black vote. So, I started sharing with a number of conservative groups.

This led to my attending rallies during the Trump campaign where I was asked and accepted the role of giving the invocation for both then candidates President Trump and Vice President Mike Pence. This was truly a privilege and honor. Once President Trump was elected, I served on the Black Voices for Trump Advisory Board.

Also, I have had the distinct honor of testifying before congress with the Subcommittee of Constitution, Civil Rights, and Civil Liberties of the Judiciary Committee regarding the following hearings—May 19, 2021, Continuing Injustice: The Centennial of the Tulsa-Greenwood Race Massacre; and then on February 4, 2022, Examining the History and Importance of "Lift Every Voice and Sing."

Clarence with then candidate President Donald Trump -2016

Clarence with Vice President Mike Pence – October 2018

Speaker at Civitas Conservative Leadership Conference; Raleigh, NC, March 28, 2014

Young Americans for Liberty - January 2016

Clarence at Greensboro City Council Meeting in support to HB2 bill

*Clarence receives the 2021
N.C. Republican Party Hall of Fame J.E. Broyhill Award
Presented by Chief Justice Paul Newby – December 2021*

POLITICAL

THE FREDERICK DOUGLASS FOUNDATION

WHO WAS FREDERICK Douglass? For those of you who are unfamiliar, he was a former slave that became one of the great American anti-slave leaders. He was an Abolitionist, suffragist, author, editor, and diplomat. He taught himself how to read and write. During the American Civil War he served as an advisor to Abraham Lincoln to include advising him on the Emancipation Proclamation. He also received appointments from Presidents Grant, Hayes, Garfield and Harrison. One would say he was the original civil rights leader.

In addition to traveling around the country to help bridge the gap of any divide that prevents the healing of America, I am currently the President of the Frederick Douglass Foundation of North Carolina. A national grass roots public and education organization which brings the sanctity of free market and limited government ideas to bear on the hardest problems facing our nation. We are a collection of proactive individuals committed to developing innovative and new approaches to today's problems with the assistance of elected officials, scholars from universities and colleges and com-munity activists.

Our Goals: Educate, Enhance and Empower

- By being a liaison to Black Faith Based organizations, Conservative candidates, parties and elected officials.
- We will reach out to educate the social, cultural, spiritual and civic rights needs of our nation.
- We will train political workers, volunteers and candidates as leaders in the political arena.
- Provide tools for improving the economic status of individuals, families and businesses within the targeted communities, thus enhancing the quality of life.
- Assist families in their efforts to remain safe and self-sufficient through education and training.
- Develop community engagement projects that educate the community on housing, medical information, job training projects and literacy development.

I used to work with a guy by the name of Kevin Daniels. Kevin was the first president of The Frederick Douglass Foundation of North Carolina— When an opportunity arose to go with Governor Pat McCrory's office, Kevin left his position with The Frederick Douglass Foundation.

I met Kevin during my time as Chairman of the North Carolina Martin Luther King Jr. Commission. After my tenure on the commission in 2016, I was then appointed to the position of President of the Frederick Douglass Foundation of North Carolina in 2017 by Reverend Dean Nelson, one of the founding members of the Frederick Douglass Foundation national organization. Kevin Daniels and Reverend Dean Nelson have been great sources for information and support for the North Carolina Chapter.

When I became president of the North Carolina chapter, having read the history of Ray Kroc, I envisioned the organization would operate the way Ray Kroc did McDonald's. I saw The Frederick Douglass Foundation as a change maker, all over the United States.

I've seen The Frederick Douglass Foundation as a tool that can be used, especially for the underserved people; the people whose voices are not heard. What if we can raise a group of people who are members of The Frederick Douglass Foundation, and whatever cause we need to speak on about freedom, liberty, and justice for all, we have the numbers and we can change things. Whether in a political arena or private sector, someone needs to stand up for the underserved. Things are going on in this country right now that shouldn't be, but they are because nobody's speaking for those people. We're working toward making sure their voices are heard.

Any kind of discrimination whatsoever should be made public. We are teaching more people about character, financial literacy, and understanding how to prioritize your needs before your wants. Many fundamental things that need to be taught in our community are not taught in the school system. We have a responsibility to teach them.

Pastors have a responsibility for their flock to share with them not only the gospel but how to be a better person as a Christian. I feel like God has put me in a position to share those things with people. I hear so many people right now talking about how dangerous it is to be driving as a Black person. At the same time, it's considerably more dangerous for that baby in their mother's womb, where they can't defend themselves. Yet in Chicago and Detroit, we are killing each other.

In the final analysis, what I would want to happen is for us to understand how valuable our lives are as a race of people. It's a shame and disgrace that we don't understand it's not who we are if we don't know whose we are. God has told me who I am. So, no man or woman can say that I'm any less than anyone. There is a self-consciousness of God, who created us in His image.

I notice that people tend to separate "Black leaders" from their cause in the Black community. I found that when that leader is no longer there for whatever reason, like what happened to Dr. King, the cause loses its focus. This is what happened to the civil rights movement after his demise. We need to look strategically at how we can move things forward.

The Frederick Douglass Foundation of North Carolina is a member of the NC Republican Party Central Committee. In 2021, I became the National spokesman for the Frederick Douglass Foundation. It's amazing how God opens doors. We need to be aware of those trying to make America look like it did fifty years ago. It is not the same America that Frederick Douglass once lived in. We have these examples of how America has progressed, even though we're an imperfect country.

Although we have people dying to come here, we have those playing the race card for profit reasons. I will always stand in opposition to anyone who wants us back in the era of Jim Crow. We've come out of slavery and will never go back. Yet the slavery that many want to put us in is economic bondage. I encourage people to read and study the Roman Empire—how it began and ended. This history parallels what's happening in America, and for those who recognize it, we need to move forward and not retreat.

Chapter 3

SIT IN

It started on February 1, 1960. My participation began on Tuesday, February 2, 1960.

I got up that morning, went to A&T for some classes, and went down to the F.D. Bluford Library. There was a library upstairs, and a lounge downstairs. While I was sitting in the lounge that day, Ezell Blair came in and told me what he and his friends had done the first day. I had no idea what had gone on because I stayed off-campus. When he asked me if I would like to participate, I told him yes, I wanted to get involved. "If they serve us, I will pay for the meal," explained Ezell. It is a good thing that he offered because I didn't have any money whatsoever. And needless to say, he owes me a meal because we never ate at the counter.

We left A&T and walked to downtown Greensboro. Elm Street divided the east side from the west side of town. We left from the east side of A&T, the east side of Market Street, and walked to Woolworth's at Elm Street.

Sitting from left: Joseph McNeil, Franklin McCain, Billy Smith, and Clarence Henderson on second day of sit-ins, Woolworth, Greensboro, February 2, 1960
Photo by News & Record Staff, © News & Record
Clarence in front of mural at NC A&T State University campus food court

We proceeded to walk into the lunch counter, and then I took a seat. One of the things, you don't see on the second day is Ezell Blair or David Richmond. They were two of the original guys sitting at the counter the first day. They were there and available just in case we were arrested. I did not know that was the plan until later. They were instructed if we were locked up to call Ralph Johns to make him aware that we had been put in jail

Ralph Johns tried to get some of the A&T students to participate in some type of movement for many years because we were being mistreated. Ralph Johns owned a clothing store within walking distance of A&T's campus. A lot of guys bought clothes from him. And he had been talking to several students before and never got anything started. And then the guy you see at the beginning, Joseph

McNeil, the first guy you see sitting at the lunch counter with me, he had gone, and Ralph Johns had talked with him about it. And he said, "We're going to do something about it." But I think the straw that broke the camel's back was when Joseph McNeil got back from Christmas vacation in December. It was about two in the morning, and there was a restaurant in the bus station, and he was hungry, so he asked to be served. But they wouldn't help him. And so he went back and said, "Guys, it's time for us to stop talking and start doing." And that's how they got involved.

Ralph Johns was a Syrian, a very unusual guy in that he was involved in a lot of stuff. It became so rough for him in Greensboro that he left. He eventually moved out to California. He was in a couple of movies. He was known for getting inside of places without paying to get into the sites. There is a picture of him at a championship boxing match and inside the ring, which you know as a spectator that doesn't happen.

He was born in Newcastle, Pennsylvania, in 1916. And he served in the army. He was an actor in movies during the thirties, but he settled in Greensboro. He started to invoke, subtly, that the Black community needed to do something about being heard. He was the one who planted the seed.

On February 2, 1960, I had on casual attire. I wore a jacket with a hood, dressed like I was going to class. There was one guy there, McCain, who had on his ROTC uniform. All freshman students had to take one year of ROTC during that time. It was a requirement. Other than Franklin McCain, we all just dressed in regular clothing.

It was in the morning before lunch when we got there, but we were ignored. It was like we were invisible. Nobody would talk with us at all, even though one of the employees was a Black guy. You can see him in the picture. He worked behind the counter. I mean, I don't know whether he washed dishes or what he did, but he was there also. The Woolworth employees acted as if we did not even exist. We caught them off guard because they didn't realize what was going on. I guess they may have thought that since nothing happened the first day, maybe that would end it. But when we came back with more people on the second day than on the first day, that's when things started to change.

Greensboro has always been a kind of middle-of-the-road city, and if you're not a part of the clique, you're being ignored. And it's still the same way now where you have certain people who have run Greensboro for several years. It goes from one family to another, like that. The Cone Brothers, who owned Cone Mills—Cone Hospital was named after them. There was normalcy that Black people were sup-posed to act a certain way. In other words, stay in your place. And that was sort of like an understanding that we were second-class citizens. And so, for so long as we didn't rock the boat, then nothing happened. To prove how far Greensboro was behind, we saw other lunch counters integrated before our very own. It all started here, but we were not the first to change.

The local manager of Woolworth's reached out to his boss in New Jersey to find out what to do, but he told him that he was on his own and would stand by his decision. It was up to him. There was a series of meetings trying to get people to come together about the sit-in. But there was not an agreement. They wanted to stop the sit-in, and then negotiate. But we had this momentum going. If we lost it, then we probably would never gain it back.

And another unusual thing about Woolworth's is that everybody was able to shop the same way in that it was a general store where all people went in and out. So, we went in, and looked at various items to purchase, picked out what we wanted, and took it to the cashier to pay for it. The only two places were downstairs with the bathrooms and water fountains and the upstairs and lunch counter, where they sepa-rated us by race. And that had gone on for many years. Had the civil rights movement not started, I don't know when that lunch counter would have been integrated. But Dr. King even made a statement that we were an integral part of breaking the color barrier and tearing down the laws of Jim Crow.

There was no violence on that day. We only suffered threats and name-calling. After that there were people on each side of the street. You had people who were against the movement, and on the other side, you had people who were for the movement. So, it was sort of like they had lined up on one side versus the other side. And that's how it went on for that length of time. What changed it probably was not just the movement, but also the economic impact it had on Greensboro. That's what changed it. Because the thing that we looked at is that the move-ment had to be a nonviolent movement from the standpoint of the Black community. We would not commit any violence no matter what they did to us. If they said they were going to harm us, we would obey the law even if it meant going to jail. It would be done peacefully and we would not resist. And some of us did go to jail. I didn't go to jail, but some people did. The atmosphere was just a quiet resolve that we were going to sit there until change occurred.

Many of us brought our books, and we would sit there at the counter and study because they were not serving food. Woolworth's had decided that they were living according to their rules and regulations and they would not help us. I later read of the financial impact that was made. And you must remember this was in 1960. It cost the store some $200,000, which would be equivalent to one or two million when you look at inflation. It wasn't just us four at the counter. The store was packed, filled with Black and White people who refused to leave. They couldn't sell any of their food at that point in time. A lot of people had stopped coming because of the sit-in movement.

The sit-in started on February first, and it ended on July 26, 1960. There were some breaks in between—some intervals for a negotiation. And then there was one break when they put the bomb threat out. Then they evacuated the store. But again, something that's not shown and not talked about; we were not acting like the victims. We were acting like overcomers. We had the tenacity, the will to see this thing through. So, the idea was to compete rather than compare. God says, it's not where you start; it's where you finish. It's where you end! Where you come from, then where you're going. It's not what's behind you nor in front of you. It's what's in you.

The two people I knew were Ezell Blair and David Richmond. I met David when I was in seventh grade. He married this young lady who I had known since the first grade. And when I was in the band, she was a majorette.

I was not in touch with Joseph McNeil and Franklin McCain. Now, each one of those guys stayed in touch because they stayed on campus together. I have never known anything about campus life. I just could not afford it. And so, as far as me having a conversation with any of those guys, I didn't. Sitting at the counter, I had a conversation with the guy sitting right next to me, Billy Smith. Ironically, Billy moved next door to my wife's aunt in Whitsett, North Carolina. He had retired from the military. He called me and wanted me to visit. But before I could get out there, he had gotten sick and had moved back to Virginia. Soon thereafter, he passed away.

The four of us were sitting there; three of us were freshmen, and Billy was a senior. But that shows you how they went back to campus to recruit other people and get others involved. That step was terrific, but I'm sure there were some people who turned them down for whatever reason. Franklin McCain has passed away. David Richmond, one of the guys on the first day, is deceased now. Ezell Blair and Joseph McNeil are both still alive. I speak periodically to Ezell. He lives in the Massachusetts area, and he's since changed his name to Jibreel Khazan. Every time I talk to him, I never think to ask him why he changed his name.

We were not afraid to ask questions. And what you have now are certain things that are off-limits. So, I'm always of the "You know, let's just have a discussion." One of the significant differences right now is that there are certain things you're not supposed to say, you can't know. Well, how do you learn about people? How do you get to know them unless you sit down and have conversations?

There have always been labels and stigmas that have been applied to Black people. My aim in life is to destroy those myths. I remember when I was at A&T—the second time I went there—and a guy I took two or three classes with never paid much attention in class, yet he made excellent grades. He was brilliant and could have gone to any school of his choice, but he chose A&T only to prove he could excel no matter which college or teacher. He also wanted to prove that Historically Black Colleges and Universities (HBCU's) had the same standards of learning as any other university. Some people go there because that's the choice that they make. That's where they want to go. And so, it's a stigma that people keep trying to put on the Black race as if again to say that we are not capable of doing certain things.

My dad, for example, had a third-grade education. I never saw him work on any car that he couldn't repair, even though other guys had the certificates as a mechanic. When you look at a person's mental faculties based on their skin color, that's a total misnomer. It's not accurate at all. These are the kinds of opportunities that give us a chance to show that we can compete in any field or endeavor. So, the idea is to compete rather than compare. It's not where you start; it's where you finish. It's where you end! It's not what's behind you nor in front of you. It's what's in you.

When I was nine or ten years of age, I found out that there was no difference in the races. I was playing with the White kids, and there was nothing ever said about the color of our skin. We just played together, and we would compete against each other, playing football, basketball, baseball, and all other games. It was the adults who instilled in the kids that there was a difference. It's much like déjà vu, where the adults are doing the same thing now. Yeah. But now they have gone further, and they have started teaching this type of ideology in our schools, which is wrong. Then we seek to prove by actions that we are as well equipped as anybody else to handle any situation whatsoever.

The civil rights movement consisted of two parts. The first part was successful; however, we still have not implemented the second part. The second part is economic empowerment for us to take full advantage of the American opportunity. Part of the problem was when integration came about, some thought that was the end of racism, but it was just the beginning. There is still a need to complete the integration and economic aspects of the civil rights movement. When integration came about, a lot of people in the Black community (either consciously or subconsciously) tried to integrate into another race of people rather than integrate into the American system. It's an American, free-market capitalistic system. An understanding of how that system works is a crucial component of absolute freedom. Understanding things like the economic quadrant, and where you fit in that quadrant whether you are an employee, self-employed, business owner, or an investor. After all these years, there is still a disconnect, and we still don't understand it now.

So, again, what I am pushing now is economic empowerment. The concern then is the same now—that Little Johnny can't read. It is not about Little Johnny's skin color as much as it is about his ability to be productive in society! I was taught to do the best I could, to be very competitive in all the things that we did, because the saying was that "we had to be better than for them to see us as being equal," and we understood that. For the most part, whenever we did things, we did them as unto the Lord, the best we could to prove that we had the skill set.

I came up under what I call classical education, where we were taught to compete rather than compare. We were taught facts over feelings. Obviously, that worked well for us because if we had gone according to emotions, we would have shrunk away from being called out by any one of the racist names when we were growing up. It was nothing to be walking down the street and somebody would drive by yelling out a racial slur or name. I don't need anyone telling me that they grew up in the north and did not experience racism. I lived in New York, and the same things that were happening in Greensboro happened there. The difference was the larger population in New York made it seem like it was not as prevalent.

At the lunch counter in Woolworth's, the Ku Klux Klan came in to bully us, but we still sat. It was a movement of hundreds of people. The Black community spoke without speaking that we were going to stand fast. We were going to hold on until a change occurred. That's when they realized that unless integration happened, they would be dealing with the situation from then on. When the students at A&T went home for summer break, they assumed that it would end, but Dudley high schoolers took over and kept the sit-in movement going until it broke the back of Jim Crow in Greensboro.

AGENDA VS. PRINCIPLE-DRIVEN MOVEMENTS

The Black Lives Matter (BLM) movement is not the same as the sit-in movement. There is a difference in the response in that BLM looks at it by any means necessary. BLM is tearing down what we built by burning buildings, causing mayhem, and setting fire to police cars. You won't see any violence or destruction in the sit-in movement. Ours was to build up. Ours proved that we understood that we were the same as anyone else. And instead of us trying to make a statement like, "I'm as good as," we showed by action that we were as good as. And like I said with Ezell, if a meal would be served like anybody else, we expected that we would pay for it. And so, when we sat at that lunch counter, we knew that if they were serving us, it was not going to be a free meal.

During that sit-in, what you saw was students sitting, talking to each other, having great conversations, but no violence occurring whatsoever. The other thing it taught me is that, and I've looked back at history, I don't see the history where any movement started with older people. It's always been with younger people.

The movement ended on July 25, 1960. There were three phases to the movement. The first people to integrate the counter were people who worked there. It was not even the students. A strange phenomenon is that I never ate there. I would go out to eat, but Woolworth's was never on my mind. I just wanted the right to eat there. When I was in school, we were taught history. Learning how a bill becomes law and civics and geography subjects trained me to be a good citizen. In other words, I understood how America works. At that time, most people in America had some working knowledge of how America works. And far too many people now don't have a working knowledge. Many people believe that America started at the time that they were born.

HOW DOES AMERICA WORK?

AMERICA WORKS FROM an economic standpoint. We have been under the free-market capitalistic system, which shows that you can fail your way to success. Two examples of this are Thomas Edison (1,000 unsuccessful attempts) and Booker T. Washington (four times before successful brick building). And the better you understand that system, the better chance you have of succeeding. There's a big difference between working for somebody and having somebody work for you, between being an employee versus an employer. For a profitable employee to be advantageous to an employer, they have to be worth four times as much as the salary being paid. You have people right now who think they are supposed to get paid, basically, as much as the owner is paid.

When I was growing up, the person who didn't make enough money went and looked for another job or worked two jobs. I grew up with several people who worked two jobs at a time. They had figured out what they wanted to improve their lot in life. It wasn't up to an employer or the government. It was up to them. Welfare today is not what it was when I was growing up. It was intended to be only for a brief time to get on one's feet, not to be a lifestyle.

And families helped each other out, and the church would help families out with problems. One person may see another family in need and buy groceries and clothes for them. So, it was a close-knit community that helped each other out. And in a lot of ways, we have lost that.

Growing up, you had parents who were head of the household. Now, from a monetary point of view, you have the government as the head of the family with welfare. My dad figured out that he would make very little money because of his education if he went into the factory. So, that's when he decided that he would become self-employed. And as much money as his hand could turn, that's how much money he made. That's where I picked up, going into business myself and developing a business system.

Those things should be taught in our education system, but today's students are not being trained in this area of expertise. America would be so much more successful if it taught how America works. Our education system needs to be revamped. Many courses they're teaching should be voluntary and not requirements, because they don't help everybody with the process to life. When I was going to school, a male had to take shop. I learned how to build things, how to do wood crafting. A female had to take home economics, which taught how to cook and do various other things around the home like budgets which are not being taught now.

What has happened to America is that there have been decades of repetitive failure in our school system to understand that it's not what America owes you. It's not what America can do for you, but what you can do for America, as stated by Former President Kennedy. Does the question become what will be said about a person? Because we would always talk about what it means to be a good citizen and to have allegiance to our country.

Every day, I remember acknowledging the flag. We went out and put the flag up on the flagpole. It was an allegiance to this country like I'd never seen before. We no longer have that kind of allegiance from someone who would even think about kneeling to our flag-kneeling before the flag was unheard of as a kid. Things have changed considerably. I'm not sure how many people understand how great this country is, even though it is an ever-evolving country many don't acknowledge as the transitional process in America. We went from the Dark Ages, if you will, to a point now where people are going back, trying to look for something that doesn't exist. You have to be careful about history.

If we don't know about it, we have to be careful not to go there again because of what happened. People who owned slaves may have relatives who are still alive. But none of them own slaves. How do we hold them accountable? We were fighting that we wouldn't be judged by the color of our skin but by the content of our character, and right now, schools have reversed that. The narrative today has been changed, and our educational system is teaching the Black community to judge White people by the color of their skin and not the content of their character.

RESPONSIBILITY

I BELIEVE WE should defend our country when we're doing the right thing. But we should also speak out against our government when they're doing wrong things. When I say speak out for doing the bad things we did as a nation, we brought to the public square an issue that the Constitution says we have the right to do so long as we peaceably assemble. The same thing goes with free speech; the right to have free speech. We not only understood our rights, but we also took responsibility for our rights. We took responsibility for ourselves as I did on my first job. I must have been fifteen years of age.

One of the jobs I had was bagging groceries on the weekend for five dollars. One of the other jobs I worked was cleaning dried mortar off bricks using a hatchet. No job was beneath us because we were looking to make money any way we could, as long as it was legal. I just wanted a job. I've worked an array of jobs, from bagging groceries, being a janitor in a school system, doing construction work, whatever was available.

I went from being what you would call underqualified, and I got to the point where I was even overqualified after I got my degree. Because it was said to me so many times, "You have come here looking for a job, and you're overqualified. I know that if I hire you and you find a better job, you're going to leave." And my statement, always, to that was "You would do the same thing. So, what you're accusing me of is the same thing that you would do." It was used against me all those years. But I never thought it would result in a protest because they didn't hire me.

This thing about crying out about discrimination all the time was unheard of when it came to income. There's always a way where you can generate income legally. If it's cutting yards, I've done that. I even, for a short time, had a janitorial service. I've never been afraid of work. I've always wanted to compete to prove that I could be the best at what I was doing. Don't tell me what I can't do. I may not do it as well as the other person, but I'll get the job done. That's always been my motto.

I ran so many people's businesses before running a business of my own. The Black community doesn't understand how valuable we are; White people will have us take care of their babies, work at their companies, and manage their businesses, but when it comes down to us doing it ourselves, there's a big difference. I remember Doug Williams, who was the first Black quarterback for the Washington Redskins to win the Super Bowl. He thought he would get all these commercials and make a bunch of money. They ignored the guy.

James Brown said, "I don't want nobody to give me nothing; just open the door and I'll get it myself." My thought process is "You don't have to open the door for me; I'll open the door myself." So it has made us a stronger people. Honestly, we are the strongest people in America because of the things we've gone through. Whereby other people may commit suicide or do all kinds of things, we have shown our capabilities and will find a way. Again, my father went from being a farmer to owning his own business with no training whatsoever.

I came out of a family that was comprised of my mother, father and two brothers. I'm the only one out of that immediate family who graduated college. But everybody in my family did well, as far as I'm concerned. My oldest brother became a policeman for the Greensboro Police Department for seventeen years. And my middle brother, after he came out of the Navy, was a supervisor at a Giant Food in Washington, DC. And we all three went in business together at one point in time in Greensboro. So, we just understood that we could do it. It's a matter of how bad you want it and what price you are willing to pay.

The same thing goes back to the civil rights movement. I'm willing to pay whatever price it is to live as a citizen like anybody else in the United States. I am opposed to somebody saying that based on my skin color, I'm not allowed to do this or that. There have been several events like getting on a bus in Greensboro, North Carolina, and going to New Jersey to work during the summer to buy clothing for school and having to stand up, not because there weren't any seats on the bus, but there were no seats in the back of the bus. So, I've seen that all my early life.

It is a sad situation when people are primarily talking about racism and critical race theory, et cetera, when there are so many other important things. Too often we allow others to occupy our minds. Instead of being individual thinkers, we become collective thinkers, allowing somebody to indoctrinate us by telling us what we can or cannot do.

The entire story needs be told about the Sit-in Movement, just like other history about the Black community. We did have other races of people participating, even though it was a few. The thing that stands out is that it was a peaceful movement. When I see people right now talking about peaceful demonstrations last year with the vandalism and burning of federal buildings, it tells me that they don't know what a peaceful movement consists of. They are one of the most powerful tools you can use because they bring attention. The picture of us at that counter has been seen worldwide, showing the way to protest.

Foreign people and foreign nationalities have interviewed me about the sit-in and my participation. So, that picture went all over the world. I've seen it in just about every magazine you can think of because of the action activity it showed about what America looked like, the hidden secret of America, which has now been brought to the forefront. So, the question becomes, now, what are you going to do about it?

Later on, the sit-in proved that our Declaration of Independence, our Constitution, and our Bill of Rights are not just pieces of paper with words on them. Those words can be lived out. If we have people representing us who are going to adhere to those laws and rules and regulations, you will find fairness, equality, and right to life and liberty, and then see what happens for us all.

PRESIDENTIALLY RECOGNIZED

How other people see me and how I see myself is different. People call me a civil rights hero and an activist. I have never seen myself like that. I have just been willing to speak out about something I believe in. If I believe in it, will I be willing to stand up for it? That courage is necessary for this freedom. Far too many people have cut their teeth on the comfort of security. And far too many people have cut their teeth on the true grit of courage that's required for freedom's sake. Those of us who have cut our teeth on the courage needed for freedom's sake owe it to the others to reach back and tell them what we went through to carry them over.

I have been fortunate to have been recognized by the President on two occasions. During Black History Month, 2019, the President recognized the first woman released under his criminal justice reform bill along with civil rights activist Bob Woodard and me. The second acknowledgment was on July 4th, 2019, at his Salute to America Celebration.

Black History Month - February 2019

Black History Month - February 2019

86   FORGOTTEN COURAGE

Black History Month - February 2019

July 4, 2019

PRESIDENTIALLY RECOGNIZED

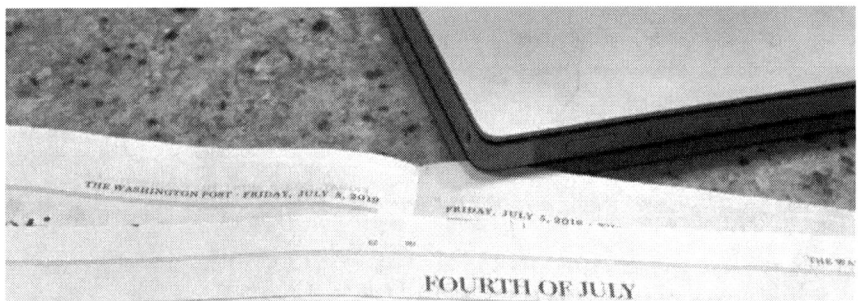

Salute to America - The Washington Post July 5, 2019

Clarence with Dr. Jerome Adams

The former Surgeon General for President Donald Trump is Dr. Jerome Adams. He came to me, and he thanked me. He said, "It is guys like you that made it possible for me to do what I've done."

*Clarence with NC Lt. Governor Mark Robinson
and GOP Texas Chair Allen West
At the NC Future Young Republicans event at the
International Civil Rights Museum in Greensboro, NC.*

Allen West said the same thing about me publicly. Countless people have conveyed the same sentiment.

It gives me that good feeling to know I participated in helping change the course of history in America for the greater good. Not to make it worse, but to make it better. Nobody can take that away from me. Some Black people are calling me the same names White people called me when I was growing up. They don't understand that I'm fighting for their freedom. It is not about the color of your skin. It's always going to be about something. If racism weren't lucrative, you wouldn't hear so much about it. As a race of people, we have to be careful not to wind up on reservations. Already, many of us live on reservations, just like the Indians do. The reservations are urban city projects run by Democratic leaders. We have paid too high a price to be caught up in victimization right now. We need to prove that we can compete. We need to prove that we can be the best in our endeavors.

Jesse Owens, again, is a prime example of being at the top of your game. He went to the Olympics and destroyed the myth about the so-called "White race aka the White man's race." And it has happened time after time. I think about people like Jackie Robinson, and how he was very peaceful in the beginning to prove that he could do what he did. But then, when he had established himself, he became very out-spoken. These athletes have opened doors for me that I can't describe.

But the most influential open door for me is that I became a born-again Christian; I saw the world differently now than I did then. As I go back and forth doing various things, I pray for direction with the Frederick Douglass Foundation. For example, the guy I travel with a lot of the time, we pray going and coming. God has opened doors that no man can close. The very idea that somebody would come to me and say, "Can I have your autograph?" Or "Can I take a picture with you?" feels crazy to me, because you won't see any selfies of me. If you see me in a picture, somebody's taken the picture, and I was there with him.

I don't do a lot of picture-taking. I've never even thought about it.

I stand on that which I've done. When I look at the Bible, I see the oldest person there in the Bible, Methuselah, but I don't see anything he did, except he was the most senior person there. So, it's not how old you are but what you do. I'm running the race, and I've kept the faith. I've got miles to go and promises to keep because I would hate to see America go back to what it was before. That would be a shame.

The greatest thing I've learned is what it means to be a leader. Nobody's a leader unless you turn around and somebody's following you. I have more places to speak today than I have time. I could go to events every week if I chose to.

Chapter 4

ADULT LIFE

CIVIL RIGHTS MOVEMENT HIJACKED

THE ENVIRONMENT IS so crucial. Men talked about Dr. King's father, and he was sitting at the table and meeting with civil rights leaders. Of course, with Dr. King and his siblings running around the house, and hearing various things, I think it led him to do the things he did. He was well prepared when God called him out to lead the civil rights movement. Dr. King was elected to pastor Drexel Baptist Church. The leadership did not realize they were bringing somebody in as controversial as Dr. King was. And so, it opened the door for the opportunity for the civil rights movement.

The challenges that we've had with the civil rights movement are that we have not been able to relinquish the past, and we continue to have other people tell us what we should or should not do. The second part of it, which has never been started or completed, is economic empowerment. Once you move into the area of economic empowerment, it changes things and positions you to take advantage of the free market capitalistic system that America operates under, which most people don't understand.

I was very fortunate to be well versed in that area of expertise because I spent almost thirty years in business doing mortgages, investments, and insurance. I truly understand how money works and how people can take whatever amount of money they have coming to their household and budget it out and then have it go that much further. Oftentimes people tend to buy what they want and beg for what they need.

In my opinion, civil rights opened up the avenue for people of all races or creeds or colors to have equality to go into business or to make money. It opened the door by exposing what was going on in America. It opened the door to test the laws of this country. Whether or not our charters of freedom, including the Declaration of Independence, the Constitution, and the Bill of Rights, were merely pieces of paper, or were they indeed the law of the land? We have found that most people only see them as words.

Right now, I head up this committee for Justice Newby, and the concentration is on how the judicial system is perceived, especially in the Black community. Many say it's not fair and equitable. It's a fascinating time now in my life, and that's what drives me—to be able to effect change and not just sit on the sidelines and allow the world to pass. I've just been put into situations where I have a voice that could be heard, because I sit on the central committee for the Republican Party now, where I bring forth issues that probably would never have been talked about before. After all, they don't live in those areas and don't know what those issues are. I make sure that the underserved community's voices are heard because they are a valuable part of the American fabric of our communities and society.

God, using Moses, took his people out of Egypt and not just out of Egypt, but the Egyptians were so glad and elated they were leaving that they gave them possessions they didn't have before. That's where we are at this point. We have the opportunity to advance the cause more significantly than ever before. But we need to understand how it is to be done because the Bible says that the wealth of the unjust is laid out for the just, but it's only going to be transferred, based on us doing the right thing according to what thus says the Lord. It's like when the Holy Spirit touches you; you're never the same. God is saying, "I can't get to you because I can't get through you."

The first thing that Christians need to understand is that in the LBGTQ community, God has turned them over to a reprobate mind. They're not clothed in their right mind, and we need to understand how we need to operate with that. First and foremost, we need to pray for them, but we also need to call things out according to the truth. There are only two sexes, and we should not allow them to force us into saying things that are not true. We've had, over the years, people who have been martyred because they would not deny their true convictions. We have to be the same way now, and when we do that, God begins to change things.

The LBGTQ have hijacked the civil rights movement and advanced it one step further. They've gotten themselves in key positions so that when they speak, it has a lot of impact. We have just stood on the sidelines and not let our voices be heard. We thought the civil rights movement, in many ways, had ended, but it seems like the LBGTQ are using it. We still have to deal with it now because, see, freedom is not free, and it always has to be defended. We are either moving back toward King George III or protecting our freedom. God has given each person an individual voice to speak out. Others are trying to make us a collective when we're individuals. We need to always see what has happened in this country because we have all these different kinds of justice, social justice, and things. It's either just, or it's unjust. The broader you define an issue, the more difficult it is to defend the true definition of what it is. We also see where people want to redefine words, where up is down and down is up. But we need to deal with the true meaning of a word from its origin, which removes many controversies.

Frederick Douglass Foundation in support of Jack the Baker in Washington DC, in 2017. Reverend Dean Nelson is at the podium.

EDUCATIONAL SYSTEM

WE'VE ALLOWED OUR educational system to change. My experience was classical education, where we understood how to debate and defend the thought processes. Today, kids are indoctrinated and taught what to think instead of how to think, which has caused a significant problem within this country.

I hear some people saying, "Well, this is how I feel about my situation." I don't want to know how you feel until I understand what you think, and then, you can tell me why you think the way you think. The thinking may be flawed and maybe it's not the truth, because feelings change regularly, but the facts do not change.

When schools were segregated, and then they became integrated, "First they wouldn't let us in; and now, they won't let us out!" That system has failed us, and parents have the opportunity to look at what is best for their children. And we have misnamed what you want to call the school as a choice, but it actually should be the parents' choice; the public education system says that the charter schools are taking away their monies, but those monies don't belong to them. Those are tax dollars, and they should go where it's best suited to educate our children. Educated people will have the most incredible opportunity to remain free instead of those who are not educated.

There is a young lady who is a part of our taskforce, and when she transferred her kids from public to charter schools, it made all of the difference in the world. So you can't convince her because she's had the experience that had she not had the opportunity to have her kids participate in parents' choice, where would her kids be today? There were kids in Washington, DC, who had received scholarships to schools that their parents had chosen, and Barack Obama blocked it. It would be interesting to know where those kids are now versus where they probably could have been having had a better opportunity for education.

Clarence has a discussion with Dr. Ben Carson at Piedmont Classical High School in Brown Summit NC on October 28, 2020 in reference to Urban Opportunities and Solutions

Chapter 5

LIFE EXPERIENCES

ECONOMIC EMPOWERMENT

MOST OF US do not even know what economic empowerment is. When you mention the financial quadrant, not many have an idea of what that is or could give a definition of it; whether you are on the left side of the equation or the right side, whether you are an employee or self-employed, or you are a business owner or an investor.

At one point, it was said, "If you're an employee, you must be worth at least four times as much as the salary that they're paying you." And this means that we need more Blacks participating in the free-market capitalistic system as business owners. But we must understand how it works. When you start as a business owner, you wear two hats, one as the employee and the other as an employer, and you have to evaluate if you the employer would hire yourself as an employee to work for you. And if you did hire yourself as an employee, would you keep yourself on board based upon the point of productivity required? And so, it's an unknown. I don't know of any place that they teach it in the school system.

There are ways other than expensive universities where you can learn the American success system, whether financial or business.

One of the things you can do is research to find that out and look around to see who would offer any advice that might be in the business for themselves or attend a community college. One of the things that we don't do enough is to invest our time into this kind of situation, where you go and look. Being able to sit under a person who genuinely understands the free-market capitalistic system and is willing to have you or share that with you is invaluable. But we have to understand the difference between spending time and investing time.

We need to understand the difference between owning a business, managing someone else's business, and working in someone else's business. Through the years, people who own their businesses have used us to run their businesses, and they enjoy the fruits of our labor. While they're out for vacation and whatever, we are busy running their businesses. I think about the quality of time that we lose out on simply because we don't quite understand information. So the history is out there. It's just that we have to research that. I can't remember who said it, but they said, "If you don't want Blacks to know how to get the information, put it in a book, and they won't read it." It's not that we don't read, but that we won't read.

That's unfortunate, and we've got to wake our people up and share with them how to progress. It goes back to a slavery mentality where you are defined by being in the house or the field. And the house was taught that the pie is a zero-sum pie. So it would be best if you kept that portion that you have accumulated. Keep that portion that's possible for you on your side because there's not enough to go around. And so, again, the information disseminated to the Black population is not totally what it should be. We're so focused on ourselves, and when you talk to a young man today, he will say that "I'm going to become a professional basketball player or enter into the entertainment field." When you ask them what their backup plan is, they don't have one.

Look out across the spectrum of professionals in the athletic field or the entertainment field. How many of those individuals have acquired money and kept it? It usually passes through their hands and they wind up penniless. For example, I look at a former boxing champ and where he is at this point, and all the money has passed through his hands. And it's just a sad situation that God gifted us with these talents, and we allow ourselves to be used and abused because we don't research and get the information to be well-rounded. In the professional arena, you often look at people who make the most money as agents, and they don't have to put themselves in harm's way. We're so busy with the social side of justice that we can't see, for lack of a better word, the monetary side of justice. Because, even as the Bible says, "A laborer is worthy of his hire." We need to consider that.

I've often wondered about our fundamental role in the National Basketball Association (NBA). It is a league that has predominantly Black players. We have dominated the NBA for so many years, but why don't we have more Black owners in the NBA. If they don't give us ownership, we need to start our own professional league and compete against them. A few years ago, they had the NBA and American Basketball Association (ABA). Initially they did not merge because the NBA did not see the ABA as a viable part of professional basketball. But then they finally did merge. We have to begin to think outside the box, look at the opportunities, and take advantage of those options.

I can't say precisely why economic empowerment is not talked about, except that we don't have a working knowledge of it. As I said before, we have this crowd mentality. It's like, "I'm afraid that Dr. Paul Brintley will get ahead of me. So the information I have, I won't share with him." No, what I have to do is find out how I can better Dr. Paul and how he can better me. With that in mind, it is not about who is better, but that I am my best.

My youngest daughter, who lives in Georgia, has told me about the number of times she's gone to professional athletes to ask them to reach back and share information with our young men. She constantly reminds me of their response and how they say, "I don't have time." They refuse to do it, which is a sad reality because we all have had assistance from someplace. We need to learn how to build a legacy within the Black community with a monetary gift. If we have anything that needs to be done in the United States, it is how many Blacks could pull their money together and make a significant difference. We have to realize that and start to look at how America works. We've been, for so many years, told all the bad things about America, but we have to look around and see what success looks like and what the formula for success is. We have missed out for the most part throughout the years from the time that America was started.

ANYONE CAN BE A BUSINESS OWNER.

Now, I'll give you an example. I have a friend who started with a lawn mower business, cutting people's grass, and then the business was built to the point where he had more clientele than he could take care of annually. He hired someone and started to pay commission on sales out to them as a part of their business. And then from that, he built himself two or three companies.

Black farmers of America were a massive business. But how many Black farmers do we have to participate in that arena? I talked with a friend of mine who is a farmer. And he spoke about the loans that the current administration has out there. He said, "They will tie you up, and you'll wind up with them who actually will own your farm if you're not careful." He says that there is no advantage to that loan. We have to go back to what President Ronald Reagan said, "Trust, but verify." We have to make sure that when we enter today's fields of expertise, we either work with people who have a working knowledge, or we need to have the working knowledge ourselves.

My father was a mechanic, and he owned his business. He was the best example I could get, but his three sons missed a great company right in front of them. And we didn't recognize it and approve it. My two deceased brothers knew very little about mechanics, and I probably know less than the two of them because all I saw was grease under my father's fingernails. I didn't see how he looked at how America works, and he understood that he would make very little money with his educational background. But by utilizing his God-given talents, he could make as much as his hands could move to do. He began to look at how he could generate money from other places. When cardboard was high, he would go around and comb through the dumpsters and get the cardboard. He did the same with the drink bottles. He would even see the copper prices rise and learn how to extract copper from various places. He knew how to turn a dollar. Many of us get caught up with a salary, but we don't understand how to turn a dollar. Too many times, we handicap kids by not teaching them the value of money and how to go out and earn their own money.

The franchise model is great. You have to understand how the model works because often, you have the franchise model and don't have a product or service that they are marketing. It's sort of like a pyramid scheme, so you have to know the difference between a legal franchise model and an illegal franchise model. You don't want to get caught up in a situation where you lose a bunch of money or even risk going to jail. So again, it requires that you have some expertise, or you find somebody with some expertise, a mentor. Another thing is that franchises already have a system, so you don't have to create one.

My partner and I researched and found a company where we could invest our time and energy, and I did that with A. L. Williams. It started with a football coach who started doing it part time when he looked at the financial services industry. He saw how, for example, the life insurance industry was taking advantage of their policyholders, where they had their biggest product, cash value life insurance on the market.

ANYONE CAN BE A BUSINESS OWNER.

They would attach the cash value with the life insurance policy and put it into a savings account that didn't belong to the policyholder. And to prove that out, if we borrowed money from their account and death occurred, they would subtract whatever amount of money you borrowed from that amount reduced by the cash value of that policy. Or, if death occurred, the cash values were a part of the life insurance policy face value. Knowing the difference between term insurance and cash value life insurance provided an opportunity to help policyholders maximize their investments through mutual funds These are invaluable lessons that are out there for us to learn. It's just a matter of willingness to pay the price.

STARTING A BUSINESS

FIRST AND FOREMOST, you have to have the right mindset and understand that you will make less money when you start with a business than perhaps you would have if you worked on a job. You may have to put in a bunch of hours over and above initially, but if you can survive and turn it around, you have the opportunity to generate more income than you could make as an individual, because you have those profit margins that you can build on with your company. The company I was with primarily had a plan to say that you will own that business if you treat it as your own. It was not left up to another individual, but yourself. The business already had that put in place. But when looking at owning a business, I think about the number of people who have run other people's businesses, and they wound up with only the amount of money that they made, the salary made, as opposed to what the business owner, the opportunity they would make. When you look at minimum wages, you get locked into a minimum wage that becomes the maximum wage. You cannot have guaranteed income and unlimited income.

Two, you can't have both guaranteed and unlimited income at the same time. So as that person going into business for yourself, you have to have a certain kind of mentality. Some think they need to have a job because they want to work from 9:00 to 5:00, go home, and do other things.

The history of America shows that the foundation for the entrepreneur has been laid. I'll use Henry Ford as an example. He was a visionary, and when Henry Ford decided that he wanted to build a model with eight cylinders on an eight-cylinder block, he drew it up on a sheet of paper and took it to his engineers. It wasn't something that he could do. His engineers went away and worked on it for a year, and they came back and said, "It can't be done." He said, "Yes, it can." One of the engineers committed suicide from the pressure. But what were the names of those engineers? Nobody talks about them. We talk about Henry Ford, the visionary. Those visionaries are the ones who come up with these kinds of things and work their way through them.

Being in business for yourself is a walk of faith. The advantage that I had was that I found one of those businesses where you could do it part time. You didn't have to walk away from your guaranteed income. And a lot of them right now are still working part time. Those who have been able to have more success have left the job and gone into business for themselves. Most of my time was spent in the field in the evening when people were at home. And I met with them after they got off work. And a lot of them right now, I'm sure, are still part time.

I talked to you about the guy who was an insurance agent already, an independent insurance agent, and he went into Primerica. It was A.L. Williams at that time. He was in debt. He owed $300,000, and he was worth twelve million dollars when I left the business. He sat and questioned the guy who recruited him until he truly understood how the industry worked. We had what you call kitchen table presentations, and we'd go to a kitchen table and talk to a couple about their financial situation. He was one of the best I had ever seen, but he didn't spend a whole lot of time doing that. He spent a lot of time training other people how to do it. We had to go back to understanding the difference between doing things and getting things done. That way you're able to build a company that has incentives that are far and above what you can make as an individual. I think about a guy like Bill Gates, who quit college and built what he built.

You have to look around and see what products or services that are needed or wanted. There's no need to go into a business or start a business model where no one is interested in that business or service. You must make sure that it's something that's needed. Why don't you take the fast-food industry? That was a niche where people were busy and went out and worked and maybe had thirty minutes or an hour for lunch. The fast-food industry came along. They don't always provide the best food, but they provide a service that will get you in and out as quickly as possible—a lot of research that you'd have to do about the thriving industry.

I've been asked a lot lately about investing and if it takes a lot of money to start a business. My response is, it depends. There are two ways that I know to go into business. One is you can build a business, or two, buy a business. The way I got started was the price of an insurance license, and during that time, it was thirty-five dollars. That is how I got started in the business. You can have interactions that require a lot of money, and those that don't need much money.

When you go into business, there can be a disadvantage because of the color of your skin. When I was in A.L. Williams/Primerica, I noticed that you might have White clientele who would purchase your products or services, but there would be customers who would not buy from me. But I just said that you have to dig in and find enough people to look at the color of money first instead of skin color.

At that point in time, you have to look at it from the standpoint of *some will, and some won't, so what, some are waiting.* The idea is to build an organization according to the business success model. You'd get paid seven generations deep. A.L. Williams/Primerica is a great business model. A number of people have retired and currently hold meetings and set up training for people working in this organization.

STARTING A BUSINESS

ABORTION

The only thing that matters is if you have life. I don't care what you're looking at… a house, a car, or whatever, because without life, none of them matter or have any value. When I look back at what has happened in the Black community since *Roe v. Wade*, there were some twenty million Black babies aborted, more than the population of all Black people back in 1960. When I look at what has happened to our community, it is just totally a torn-up community. Seventy-nine percent of the abortion clinics are in low-income areas. They're still using the same model to keep the Black population down because after slavery there was no way to control our destiny. One of the ways to control the people was to use abortion clinics. They continue to use them now, but most of our people are not aware of what it does to control the population and what it does to the community at large. However, it is to my delight that as of June 24, 2022, the United States Supreme Court has reversed *Roe v. Wade*. With that decision it is my hope that healing will come to this nation.

I hear all the time that the babies don't feel pain. Now they're saying the babies do feel pain. As of late, they take these baby parts and sell them.

Unfortunately, we've had situations occur that have taken advantage of the Black community.

One of the biggest things that happened in America was when Barack Obama was picked, and then he was nominated, and he became the president of the United States. His victory kept the Black community in the camp of the Democratic Party even up to this time. According to the history that I read, when he was a senator he voted to deny basic Constitutional protections for babies born alive four different times.

He was picked to be the poster child for the Black community. He is a very articulate guy who did not express anger and seemed cool under the pressure. The Democratic Party knew what they were doing. President Obama's thought process was that he was against the American system. One of the things he said was that "I don't like the Constitution because it's too restrictive." The Constitution is restrictive because it protects the people against the government because the bigger the government, the smaller the people. People don't understand that we have become more dependent on the government. "So, let's go see what the government says" is most people's first reaction to a dilemma.

Our government is not the answer to all things. For example, when they spend money on things that could be better handled by the private sector, they should use what is known as the "Yellow Page Test" and contract it out. The government should use that Yellow Page test to determine if contractors out here could do the job better than the government could do for less money, contract it out, and save a lot of money. We still find that today. The government takes so much advantage of people. It's the most effective welfare system there is. They don't produce anything. But most people want to become more and more dependent upon the government, just like we are right now. If the government says it's all right, it must be all right. That is not a true statement.

ABORTION

Ronald Reagan said, "The nine most terrifying words you can hear are 'I'm from the government, and I'm here to help.'" And that's a very true statement that their incentive is those who sit in the halls of Congress, how much money passes through their hands before they get to the place they're supposed to be sending it? It's just like these various practices they put together now; a lot of that money will incentivize people to continue to vote democratic. The Democrats see it as a meal ticket to being elected.

The Biden administration incentivized people by still giving them checks so they would vote for him. We must understand that if people are not aware, they'll be taken advantage of even today. It's all right to make this mistake the first time, but it's a person's fault for making the same mistake the second time. Now it's your fault.

The government's role should be limited. We see the government pushing these clinics, these abortion clinics in the Black community, where a Black lady is five to six times more likely to have an abortion than a White lady. Why do you think they have strategically placed these clinics in the Black neighborhood? Because those are the people in the low-income area. The Black community used to have one of the highest rates for marriage. But we don't now; we have so many single mothers, and it's gone from generation to generation, and it has become a way of life in the Black community.

I think of one person who pushed this thing: Lyndon Baines Johnson. He knew exactly what he was doing when he came up with The Great Society. And we still are feeling the results of it today because his thing was that I will have Blacks voting for democrats for the next 200 years, but he didn't use that word. He used the N-word. He was one of the greatest political strategists of all time in understanding how to keep people under control of the government.

In reducing abortions in the Black community, we can think of various organizations and organizations that started out doing that like the NAACP, but they fell by the wayside. But now we have organizations like the Frederick Douglass Foundation that can go in to help. The Frederick Douglass Foundation has a sister organization called

The Douglass Leadership Institute. We are going into churches and places like that to spread help. One of our main topics is strengthening the Black family and understanding that the free market capitalistic system does not work very well for that single parent. If they had to take that child through daycare and various other things, it might be more costly for them to go to work. It may be more expensive for them to go to work than to stay on welfare.

FAMILY STRUCTURE

In 1940, 60 percent of Black women worked as domestic servants; today, the number is down to 2.2 percent, while 60 percent hold white-collar jobs.
In 1958, 44 percent of Whites said they would move if a Black family became their next-door neighbor; today, the figure is 1 percent.
In 1964, the year the great Civil Rights Act was passed, only 18 percent of Whites claimed to have a friend who was Black; today, 86 percent say they do, while 87 percent of Blacks assert, they have White friends. http://www.brookings.edu/articles/Black-progress-how-far-weve-come-and-how-far-we-have-to-go/

THE BEST EXAMPLE when I was growing up in the Black community was that it emphasized a complete family with a mother and father. My father never considered going on welfare. He was determined to take care of himself and his family. He got up every morning and was out the door going to work and getting back at 6:00, 7:00, 8:00 at night. So, he may leave the house at 6:00 to 7:00 in the morning, depending on what job he would do. Well, he was doing mechanic work. And he didn't come back until he got the job done.

It was a different kind of mentality back then than it is now. And we fought so hard to come out of Jim Crow because we understood that education was a key, and now we have been brainwashed and going back and saying, we always need a handout. There's a difference between a handout and a hand up. My father did everything possible to turn a dollar to make sure his family was fed. We had a roof over our head, and his family was taken care of no matter the situation. My mother never worked anything but a part-time job, as I said before. And she didn't start that job until I was in the first grade. My dad was the true breadwinner of the house, and my mother stayed home and took care of the kids. And it worked out great.

There was no conscientious objector in our family. My oldest brother was called into the Army. My middle brother joined the Navy, and I was drafted into the Army. And it was more difficult at that time to get into the military than it is now. Because even if you had flat feet or something like that, they may not take you. The biggest problem in America right now is the family structure. We can begin with the men. If we go back to the family structure, the way God designed it, and look at these various professional areas like sports, you see the guy and he starts talking about his personal life—who does he talk about? He talks about his mother. But where is the father? And that is a problem. You've got this guy with this tremendous athletic ability but no man training. There's a problem.

I remember this organization said, "If you don't build boys, you'll have to mend men." And there's this movie coming out now about the big difference it makes when there's a man in a child's life versus when he's not there. It just makes such a big, big difference. We're losing out on that. I can remember at one point in time, America had different marriage laws. It had gone to the point that it had rules about marriage, because before, Blacks couldn't get married. But I remember my uncle telling me a story about the police who came to his house and locked him and his girlfriend up because they were not married. "You can't shack, you got to be married," replied the officer, but look at it now. It seems to be an honor to be a baby daddy or an award for a woman to have kids out of wedlock, and that's very unfortunate. When I look at what's ahead of us, I see the potential for any person living in America—where they can be, what they can do and achieve?

In 1940, 60 percent of employed Black women worked as domestic servants. Today, that number is down to 2.2 percent. So, we went from 60 percent down to 2.2 percent. While now, 60 percent of Black women hold white-collar jobs. Many feel like that is progress, but I do not. It's a good statistic, but it has hurt the family unit. It has made things that have occurred that are out of order. God created Adam from the dust of the ground, and he gave a job to expand the garden. And then, out of Adam, he took one of the ribs and made a woman. That is the first order, and one of the biggest challenges we have today is where are the men?

So, the family structure, if we get that right, can help many people. Oh, it will change everything. You can't convince me with anything else, because there's so much that happens inside a home when you have the husband and wife there, and they are making plans to better their family. Actions speak louder than words.

THE FUTURE

WE HAVE THE greatest potential of any country in the world. We have to protect that potential by not allowing the history of America to be rewritten. We have an excellent foundation to build on, and we have to go back to making history. So we have a system in place. It's just a matter of applying those systems, and going back to classical education where we teach the whole person in a way God designed them—spirit, soul, and body—and how to build upon each one of those things.

I understand that there is a psychological and spiritual aspect of formal education. There is a part of that where the body comes in place, where we have to stay physically active. Christians have a great responsibility. We have to get out of the four walls of the church and again be the conscience of America. We had the most remarkable example of all times with Jesus. Look at the time He spent outside the church instead of inside going about the highways and byways of life.

Each of us can be a significant influence, or we can be a negative influence. I understand as a Christian that death and life are in the power of the tongue. We all must use God's words and watch mountains move. Time hasn't changed anything, and that's what Jesus said. The people wanted more faith, and he said, "Oh, ye of little faith." If you had the faith the size of a mustard seed, you could say unto the mountain, "Be thou removed and cast into the depths of the sea, and it shall be done." What is said is as good as done. We as Christians don't understand the part that the Holy Spirit plays in a born-again person's life.

We get Jesus, but we receive the Holy Spirit, and inside of each of us who are born-again Christians, we have the entire Godhead, because it can't be separated. We need to understand that all these other things are under our feet and that we're in this world, but we're not of this world. The Bible comes from the only person who can give life, and if God is for us, who can be against us? When we're on God's side, we are in the majority, and his plan is much better than our plan. It's like what Joseph said to his brothers, "What you meant for harm, God changes for good," and we would live according to that.

Then change things. It goes back to 2 Chronicles 7:14, which says, "If my people, who are called by my name, would humble themselves, and turn from their wicked ways, and cry out, and seek me, then I will hear from heaven and heal their land." Then, we can change America and change the world. Because of all the things we have been through, we are the ones who can fix the world. But first, we have to fix ourselves. We have got to go into our communities and be very honest about people and say, "Well, what we're doing in these communities is not working. Why don't we have a paradigm shift and look at stopping the insanity of doing the same thing repeatedly, expecting different results." We use every excuse in the book, and it's not working. So, it's to our detriment. Go into the prison system, and, of course, some corruption has caused some people to be there. But for the most part, we are there because of something we did that we should not have done. And we just have to learn how to be good citizens.

I have a nephew, and growing up, he spent more time in jail than out of jail, and I told him, "If you would learn how to stay out of trouble, everything else will take care of itself." Once he was going in, and I said, "I'll tell you, you're not good at what you're doing because you keep getting caught."

AFFIRMATIVE ACTION

I THINK AFFIRMATIVE action works to our disadvantage because it is used against us psychologically. It's a proven fact that the color of one's skin has nothing to do with the intellect. Think about Dr. Ben Carson, whose mother could not read nor write, but she knew the importance of those two aspects of life, and she would have her two sons read to her. They had to study when their friends were outside playing. Look at the success stories that Dr. Carson and his brother are today.

So again, we have success models, but are we willing to follow them? Unfortunately, we have too many women who look for the bad boy. What they call a nerd is not on their radar until he lives more prosperously than anybody else. We can get caught up in looking at the exterior of a person and not looking beyond that to see their intellect. When you see a thing, call it what it is and do not get caught up in saying you can make changes within another person.

Chapter 6

PROJECTS

CONTENT OF CHARACTER™ PROGRAM

You cannot change a person. You can take a child and even a dog and cause them to do the things you want them to do, but when you're no longer around them, what kind of actions do they take? The change must come from within. Our character is so important to the trajectory of our lives.

I have written a program called the **Content of Character™** that shows that America will always look like the content of the character of its people. If a person has character, they will see themselves moving up in every area of life. Now, I presented this program to the public schools in Greensboro, North Carolina, and they didn't want any part of it. But I have also presented it to a charter school, and we're starting the process of putting that program into place. Simply put, classroom decorum should be yes ma'am, no ma'am, yes sir, no sir, and they raise their hand. Whereas often teachers may spend half the class trying to get order so they can begin to teach.

An Overview of the **Content of Character™ Program**

What Is Character?

As described in Webster's dictionary, character is an essential feature, nature; total of qualities making up individuality; moral qualities; reputation of possessing them.

It is not necessarily a person's outward appearance or how they speak that reveals their character. It is what they do, the actions they take, that reveal their **Content of Character™**.

The Content of Character™ Program is designed to raise awareness and appreciation of the life and work of Dr. Martin Luther King, Jr. within the realm of promoting good character, which will translate into our youth becoming productive citizens within our society.

> *"The function of education is to teach one to think intensively and to think critically. Intelligence plus character—that is the goal of true education."*
> - Dr. Martin Luther King, Jr.

> *"The ultimate measure of a man is not where he stands in moments of comfort and convenience, but where he stands at times of challenge and controversy."*
> - Dr. Martin Luther King, Jr.

Why Content of Character™ Program?

A free society remains free only so long as they self-govern themselves and don't infringe upon the sovereign rights of others. Each person can contribute to the free society of America by the act of self-governance. Self-governance requires the right character that recognizes rights of everyone.

Our Audience
Schools, Public and Private
Youth-based organizations

Program Modules

The **Content of Character™ Program** consists of five modules with methods for youth to participate in understanding the roles, conduct, and influence of good and bad character on society.

"America will always look like the character of its people."
- Clarence Henderson

For more information about our Content of Character™ Program visit the ClarenceHenderson.com website or please contact us at:

Clarence Henderson
Post Office Box 5816
High Point, NC 27262

MOVIE PROJECT

I'VE SHARED MY story at every opportunity that has presented itself. I met this guy by the name of Faruk Okcetin, who has some experience in the movie industry. He heard me tell my story. Kevrick McCain, who works for the Douglass Leadership Institute and The Frederick Douglass Foundation, talked about the need to tell my story, so he wrote the screenplay. Kevrick, Faruk, and I formed a partnership to start the movie project.

It is a unifying movie. We are now looking for investors who are concerned about the true story of America to be told and not rewritten…investors who are troubled about the direction this country is headed. We are excited currently to continue to move forward. Anyone seeking additional information is welcome to visit my **ClarenceHenderson.com** website for more details.

Chapter 7

REPUBLICAN NATIONAL CONVENTION SPEECH 8/26/2020

CLARENCE HENDERSON, CIVIL rights activist and president of the North Carolina chapter of the Frederick Douglass Foundation, spoke on the third night of the Republican National Convention on Aug. 26, 2020.

Greetings, my fellow Americans. I am Clarence Henderson. There have been movements that have changed the course of history. Among the most extraordinary was the Civil Rights movement. 60 years ago, segregation was legal and enforced. The simple act of sitting at a lunch counter could lead to physical harm, jail time, or worse. I know from personal experience walking into Woolworth Department Store on February 2nd, 1960, I knew it was unlike any day I had experienced before. My friends had been denied service the day before because of the color of their skin. We knew it wasn't right, but when we went back the next day, I didn't know whether I was going to come out in a vertical or prone position in handcuffs, or on a stretcher, or even in a body bag. By sitting down to order a cup of coffee, we challenged injustice.

We knew it was necessary, but we didn't know what would happen. We faced down the KKK. We were cursed at and called all kinds of names. They threatened to kill us, and some of us were arrested, but it was worth it. Our actions inspired similar protests throughout the South against racial injustice. In the end, segregation was abolished, and our country moved a step closer to true equality for all. That's what actual peaceful protest can accomplish. America isn't perfect. We're always improving. But the great thing about this country is that it's not where you come from, it's where you're going. I was born on what some would call the wrong side of the tracks. I don't even have a birth certificate. I never attended an integrated school. I'm the only one out of my immediate family who graduated from college an HBCU. I'm a military veteran and a civil rights activist, and you know what else?

I'm a Republican, and I support Donald Trump. If that sounds strange, you don't know your history. It was the Republican Party that passed the 13th Amendment abolishing slavery. It was the Republican Party that passed the 14th Amendment, giving black men citizenship. It was the Republican Party that passed the 15th Amendment, giving black men the right to vote. Freedom of thought is a powerful thing. There are Americans, voters all over the country who the media is trying to convince to conform to the same old democratic talking points. You know what that will get you? The same old results. Joe Biden had the audacity to say, if you don't vote for him, you ain't black. Well, to that, I say, if you do vote for Biden, you don't know history. Donald Trump is not a politician. He's a leader. Politicians are a dime a dozen, leaders are priceless. The record funding Trump gave HBCUs is priceless, too.

So are the record number of jobs he created for the black community and the investment he drove into our neighborhoods with tax incentives and opportunity zones. So are the lives he restored by passing Criminal Justice Reform, where 91% of the inmates released are black. These achievements demonstrate that Donald Trump truly cares about black lives. His policies show his heart. He has done more for black Americans in four years than Joe Biden has done in 50. Donald Trump is offering real and lasting change, an unprecedented opportunity to rise. A country that embraces the spirit of the Civil Rights movement of the 60s. A place where people are judged by the content of their character, their talents and abilities, not by the color of their skin.

This is the America I was fighting for 60 years ago. This is the America Donald Trump is fighting for today. Let's all join in this fight for re-electing president Trump on November 3rd. Thank you.

Chapter 8

IN THE NEWS
(ARTICLES AND OPINIONS)

GRASSROOTS SPOTLIGHT: CIVIL RIGHTS ACTIVIST CLARENCE HENDERSON

BY KATHY HARTKOPF
06/19/2015

Clarence Henderson is a FreedomWorks activist who participated in the Woolworth Sit-In in Greensboro, N.C. in 1960 and is a United States Army Veteran and retired entrepreneur. I was pleased to be able to sit down with him and talk about his experiences and views on empowerment.

What was the first political cause you rallied for?

Two years ago, I volunteered with the GOP in Greensboro. I was involved in the Woolworth Lunch Counter Sit-In. On February 1, 1960, Ezell Blair, Jr. (now Jibreel Khazan) was in a group of three black men who sat at the Woolworth lunch counter and asked to be served. On February 2, Ezell came to find me in the library of A&T University. He told me what had happened the day before and asked me to participate. I agreed to sit with them at the lunch counter.

What was the issue that was important to you?

I chose to participate in the Woolworth Lunch Counter Sit-In because of things that I had experienced all my life. Even as a child growing up, I knew there were people that treated me differently. I had seen the bathrooms labeled White and Colored. I had seen the water coolers labeled White and Colored, even though the water that came out of the two fountains looked the same. When in Woolworth's with my mother, we had ordered our lunch at the end of the lunch counter, since we were not allowed to sit at the counter. When I was eight or nine years old, I was riding my bicycle down a sidewalk. There was a white guy walking toward me. I moved all the way over to the far side of the sidewalk. The guy moved over to where I had moved and knocked me off my bicycle. It was like I was an invisible man.

How did you get involved with FreedomWorks/Empower?

The very name FreedomWorks is what I stand for myself – without freedom, what do you have? I was very impressed with Deneen Borelli, having seen her before. Deneen called and asked me to participate as a panelist in an Empower Event. [Clarence has served as a panelist at four Empower Events in North Carolina: Durham, Jacksonville, Roper, and Ahoskie.] The Durham event was moderated by Deneen Borelli.

With a bloated administrative state, a crippling federal deficit, and crushing student loan debt, what is your advice to a large percentage of millennials who are underemployed or unemployed completely?

The mind is very creative and the best hand that you can find is the one at the end of your own arm. Get together, start businesses, learn about entrepreneurship – which is the key to America. Become an apprentice, even if it is unpaid. Learn. If one of your goals is to be rich, find someone who is rich and learn from them. Do not become programmed. Always think for yourself. On subjects that matter to you, be able to substantiate or repudiate whether fact or fiction. Know the history of your country.

What is the most important issue facing the country today?

JOBS! When people make money, they will spend money and that is what drives the economy! If you let the free society do what it does, you have the free market!

How can we solve it?

By eliminating a lot of regulations such as tax codes. A lot of tax codes make no sense other than to make money. I would eliminate both the IRS and the EPA. The bottom line is that we need plain old common sense. What is the old adage: common sense is not so common?

Civil rights hero from 60s takes criticism as Trump backer

By Tom Foreman Jr., The Associated Press — Oct 24 2016

HIGH POINT, N.C. — Clarence Henderson was hailed as a hero nearly 60 years ago when as a young black man he participated in a sit-in at a segregated North Carolina lunch counter.

In 2016, he is again taking a risky stand; he is supporting Donald Trump.

And he isn't shy about it. Last month he gave the invocation at a Trump rally here, smiling as he shook the Republican candidate's hand.

"Donald Trump is certainly not a politician, and politicians are a dime a dozen, but leaders are priceless," Henderson said in an interview.

Trump is deeply unpopular in the black community. He has called on black voters to vote for him because "what the hell do you have to lose?" His support among blacks is less than the margin of error in some polls.

Henderson, 74, has been criticized for his stance, with many taking to Twitter to accuse him of abandoning the principles he fought so hard for more than half a century ago.

Henderson shrugged off the criticism, saying he isn't paying any attention to it.

And he has gotten some support from one of his fellow activists. Jabreel Khazan was one of the first four protesters to sit down at the Woolworth's lunch counter. And though he supports

Hillary Clinton, he said he had no problem with Henderson's choice. "God bless him and all of those who have a second opinion," said Khazan, whose name was Ezell Blair at the time of the protest. "We should not be a one-minded people."

Henderson attended North Carolina A&T State University, when, as an 18-year-old, he joined the original four lunch counter protesters on the second day of their protest. He could no longer live under the official segregation known as Jim Crow, he said.

"I did it because it was the right thing to do," he said.

Angry whites jeered at them, and he wondered if he and his fellow protesters would be brought out in handcuffs or on stretchers.

They were arrested, but their actions inspired similar protests throughout the south that led to the desegregation of lunch counters and other nonviolent protests against racist policies.

For a civil rights hero, he later ended up on a more unconventional political path that he credits to his father, a lifelong Republican.

"My dad, with a third-grade education, said to me, 'Well, son, you don't know what the Democratic party has done as far as blacks are concerned,'" Henderson said.

He discovered the Democrats had created and enforced Jim Crow and the Republican Party was behind the constitutional amendments that abolished slavery, granted equal protection to freed slaves and gave blacks the right to vote.

He cast his first vote for a Republican presidential candidate for George W. Bush. Henderson, who ran a financial services business for more than 25 years before retiring a decade ago, said he respected Bush's business background.

He continued voting for Republicans, even when Barack Obama stood poised to become the first black president.

"I never thought I would see a black person become the president of the United States," Henderson said. "His ideologies were different from mine. After looking at his past history, I didn't see him as a viable candidate."

This year, Trump was not Henderson's first choice for the GOP nomination. He supported Sen. Ted Cruz. But now that Trump has the nomination, Henderson said he respects his business experience, even as he acknowledges the candidate's off-the-cuff speaking style can be a problem.

"He has proved to be a leader in the business field. Has he done everything right? No, certainly not. But I think that he has more at stake than Hillary does," he said.

In his invocation at the Trump rally last month, Henderson nodded to his past.

"I stand before you as one that knows what America's all about - the good, the bad and the ugly. I would not live in any other country except America that put Jim Crow on trial and found him guilty of trying to separate the races. So I stand before you to say that we are unified," he said.

Henderson said regardless of criticism, he will vote his conscience.

"I would rather be in the minority on the side of justice than in the majority on the side of injustice, because I have lived a life where I saw there was injustice," he said.

Tom Foreman Jr., The Associated Press

1960s Activist Says 'Offensive' To Equate Transgender Claims With Racial Equality

NICOLAS MAETERLINCK/AFP/Getty

WARNER TODD HUSTON

20 May 2016

A man who appeared in one of the more famous photos from the 1960s fight for equal rights for African Americans, says that it is "offensive" and "insulting" to equate today's demand for transgender status with the drive to win blacks equal treatment under the law.

Clarence Henderson was one of the four North Carolina A&T College students who sat down at a lunch counter of a Greensboro Woolworth's in 1960 and demanded to be served. The iconic photo of the young men became one of the many touchstone images of the struggle for equal rights.

But today's battles over transgender bathrooms, Henderson says, is nothing at all like living through Jim Crow and the two do not deserve to be mentioned in the same breath.

Henderson opened his op ed at the *Charlotte Observer* with a stark assessment.

"Let us be clear: HB2 cannot be compared to the injustice of Jim Crow," Henderson wrote. "In fact, it is insulting to liken African Americans' continuing struggle for equality in America to the liberals' attempt to alter society's accepted norms."

Henderson went on to remind his readers of U.S. Attorney General Loretta Lynch's absurd declaration that North Carolina's traditional bathroom law, HB2, was somehow just like Jim Crow America. Henderson explains it simply saying, "Jim Crow laws were put into place to keep an entire race positioned as second-class citizens. HB2 simply says that men and women should use the restroom of their biological sex in government buildings and schools."

It is "highly offensive and utterly disrespectful to those families and individuals who have shed blood and lost lives to advance the cause of civil rights," he said. "I take this as a personal slap in the face because I was an active participant in the civil rights movement."

Henderson went on to list all the oppressions blacks faced in the pre-1964 civil rights era. Blacks faced dogs, water cannons, mobs, not to mention lynching and "400 years of slavery."

"We had to drink at separate water fountains, shop at different stores and even had to sit at the back of the bus, all because of the color of our skin," Henderson wrote.

Yet, transgender people today have faced no such hardships, the activist says.

In comparison, transgender individuals do not have to fight dogs, can shop anywhere and can use any water fountain. They are free to work, shop and ride the bus. And to my knowledge, they have not experienced 400 years of slavery and the ongoing fight for parity 151 years after emancipation.

His final words were cutting, indeed, not to transgender people but to Obama's Attorney General, Loretta Lynch.

IN THE NEWS (ARTICLES AND OPINIONS)

Loretta Lynch's political pandering to arouse African American interest in what has been proven to be lukewarm support for the supposed Democratic presidential candidate is an obvious attempt to elicit an emotional response. You cannot pimp the civil rights movement.

Throughout my life, I have noticed that even smart people say dumb things. And you, Ms. Lynch, have once again proven me right. Well done.

Henderson clearly has no use for the radical transgender agenda.

Follow Warner Todd Huston on Twitter @warnerthuston or email the author at igcolonel@hotmail.com

Clarence Henderson receives Order of the Long Leaf Pine

Photos by Staff Photographer Joseph Rodriguez

Mar 17, 2017

Greensboro Sit-in participant Clarence Henderson after receiving the Order of the Long Leaf Pine award from State Representative Jon Hardister at the old Guilford County Courthouse, on Friday, March 17, 2017, in Greensboro, N.C.

Clarence Henderson, a participant in the Greensboro sit-ins, received the Order of the Long Leaf Pine Friday at the old Guilford County Courthouse. The award is given by the governor to those with a proven record of extraordinary service to the state. State Rep. Jon Hardister of Greensboro presented the award to Henderson.

Photos by Staff Photographer Joseph Rodriguez

CIVIL RIGHTS ERA DEMONSTRATOR SPEAKS ON FAITH, UNITY, AND GOD-GIVEN RIGHTS

February 18, 2019 : By Drew Menard - Liberty University News Service

During a special Convocation hosted by the Helms School of Government on Monday, Liberty University students heard a firsthand account of the Civil Rights Movement and were encouraged to root their lives in faith in order to promote unity.

One of the guests was Clarence Henderson, president of The Frederick Douglass Foundation of North Carolina, who was a participant in peaceful protests in 1960. He was joined by Jeremy Hunt, leadership strategist for the Douglass Leadership Institute, who shared his insights as an activist from a younger generation. (Hunt gave a presentation on campus last year for African-American History Month.)

Henderson was an early participant in the Greensboro (N.C.) sit-ins, a series of peaceful protests where young African-Americans sat at the whites-only lunch counter at a Woolworth's diner requesting ser-vice and refusing to give up their seats after being denied. Henderson joined the original "Greensboro Four" on the second day of the nearly six-month protest.

"I am very privileged to have participated in one of the greatest movements that has happened in America," he said, expressing gratitude that he "had enough courage to participate in the things that I believed in."

Henderson explained that by protesting peacefully and understanding that "violence begets violence," he and the other men set out to "expose some of the wrong things in America."

"I had this great opportunity to participate in this principle-driven movement," he said. "An agenda-driven movement oppresses people. A principle-driven movement moves us toward freedom."

Henderson encouraged the students to be aware of their Constitutional right to participate in orderly demonstrations. Quoting the Declaration of Independence, he reminded the crowd of their "unalienable," "God-given right" to "life, liberty, and the pursuit of happiness."

"No man, no woman, no person, no entity has a right to take those rights away," he said.

Hunt emphasized the need for the church to rise up and speak with authority to help heal and fight against division.

"There are no political solutions to the human condition," Hunt said. "The only antidote to sin is the blood of Jesus Christ. Why are we (the church) so quiet to share this with the rest of the world?"

Hunt talked about the importance of being loyal to truth and righteousness, even if that means calling out people from our own ideological or political camps.

"There is no 'my truth,'" Hunt said. "There is only one truth: the truth."

The two men took time to answer questions, ranging from how to promote social harmony to the church's role in sparking change. Each centered their answers on the importance of a personal relationship with Jesus.

Henderson encouraged students to get outside "the four walls of the church" to speak with moral authority into the issues of the day and stressed the importance of prayer.

Hunt told the students to "read literature from authors that don't think like you" and to "make friends that don't think like you" in order to become more informed on the issues and strengthen their beliefs.

Students appreciated the opportunity to hear a message of unity, especially from a pioneer of civil rights.

"It was very inspirational," said senior criminal justice major Ryan Skinner. "I like how he (Henderson) said that in order to fix this (division), we all have to come and work together, to become unified."

Criminal justice senor Felix Hernandez added that Henderson's story was "eye opening."

"We didn't live it," he said. "We have heard of it (the Civil Rights Movement) but hearing it from a first-person perspective was a privilege."

Civil rights pioneer wants blacks to join GOP, says Democrats 'most afraid' of 'conservative blacks'

US

DAVE URBANSKI

FEBRUARY 21, 2018

Civil rights pioneer and unabashed conservative Clarence Henderson had a central message for those who gathered last week in Fayetteville, North Carolina, to hear him speak: Black voters should join the Republican Party. (Image source: YouTube screenshot)

Civil rights pioneer and unabashed conservative Clarence Henderson had a central message for those gathered to hear him speak in Fayetteville, North Carolina, last week: Black voters should join the Republican Party.

He also told those at the Cumberland County Republican Women's Club last Tuesday that "what the Democratic Party is most afraid of is conservative blacks," the Fayetteville Observer reported.

Henderson was part of the famous Greensboro lunch counter sit-in movement in 1960 that led to desegregating them, and he has credited the GOP with backing equal rights for black Americans. In the iconic photograph below, Henderson is in the far right seat:

Now as president of the North Carolina chapter of the Frederick Douglass Foundation — which aims to increase the number of conservative Christian blacks in the Republican ranks — Henderson said the organization's efforts also have seen success, the Observer reported.

What was Henderson's path toward conservatism?

Henderson told the Miami Herald that he credits his father, a lifelong Republican, with altering his political path.

"My dad, with a third-grade education, said to me, 'Well, son, you don't know what the Democratic Party has done as far as blacks are concerned,'" Henderson told the paper.

More from the Herald:

He discovered the Democrats had created and enforced Jim Crow and the Republican Party was behind the constitutional amendments that abolished slavery, granted equal protection to freed slaves and gave blacks the right to vote.

He cast his first vote for a Republican presidential candidate for George W. Bush. Henderson, who ran a financial services business for more than 25 years before retiring a decade ago, said he respected Bush's business background.

Where does he stand on President Donald Trump?

Henderson also has stood in support of Republican President Donald Trump, both during his campaign and after he took office — to the apparent chagrin of the mainstream media.

In this video a CNN host wondered why Henderson backed Trump in the wake of controversy over the president visiting the new Mississippi Civil Rights Museum:

And prior to the 2016 election, yet another CNN host grilled the civil rights pioneer on his support for then-candidate Trump and appeared to attempt to educate Henderson on racism — but he was having none of it.

"I come from an era of time known as Jim Crow," Henderson shot back, "and I know what racism is and what racism isn't." The grilling curiously — and abruptly — came to an end after that.

What is Glenn Beck's connection to Henderson?

After Beck's 2015 Restoring Unity rally in Birmingham, Alabama, the radio host shared that Henderson was one of the men marching next to him.

"I said, 'Why are you doing this?'" Beck recalled. "He said, 'It's time. It's just time. We have to come together or we're going to tear each other apart.' Isn't that fantastic?"

Community, Religious Leaders Gather to Support Charter School Transportation Grants

Lindsay Marchello

in CJ Exclusives

April 15, 2019

3:49PM

GREENSBORO — Community leaders, school choice advocates, and religious leaders gathered at Next Generation Academy on Monday, April 15, in support of a bill to help charter schools cover the cost of getting students to their classrooms.

The Frederick Douglass Foundation of North Carolina and Douglass Leadership Institute — nonprofits pushing for education reform — organized the event. Speakers talked about why they support a bill to make the Charter School Transportation Grant program permanent.

House Bill 199 would create a grant program giving certain charter schools money to help pay transportation costs. Charter schools that serve mostly economically disadvantaged students could apply for grants. The state would reimburse 65% of student transportation costs up to $100,000.

Rep. Jon Hardister, R-Guilford, a primary sponsor, said the bill was inspired in part by former Democratic Rep. Marcus Brandon, who helped Hardister craft a pilot program in 2017 to provide grant fund-ing for charter school transportation.

Hardister said the pilot program was successful.

"How do we know?" Hardister asked the audience. "Every dollar was spent."

Now Hardister, along with a bipartisan group of lawmakers, is trying to transition the program from pilot to permanent.

"If there is a school that has a high number of low-income students, then they can sometimes have trouble getting those students to schools. That's a problem." Hardister said. "How can students learn if they can't get to school?"

Unlike traditional public schools, charter schools get no money for transportation. While some charter schools can afford to contract with transportation companies or buy their own buses, many in low-income areas are unable to provide that transportation.

H.B. 199 would appropriate $2.5 million in recurring funds to the Department of Public Instruction to administer the charter school transportation grant program. Charter schools in which at least 50% of students are economically disadvantaged could apply for a grant.

Bishop Adrian Starks of the World Victory International Church said his mother was able to send him to a school an hour from the Bedford-Stuyvesant neighborhood in New York City, where he grew up. Starks was able to take a bus, and later the subway, to school. But many children in Guilford County don't have such access to public transportation.

Starks said he wants children in North Carolina to have the same opportunities he did while growing up, and that means being able to get to class.

"I believe this bill is moving in that direction for the right reason and the right time, and that's the reason I believe putting my name and my support behind it is of great value," Starks said. "I'm hoping that all the legislators ... will unanimously approve it, will unanimously see its value, and will unanimously choose to be on the right side."

The right side, Starks said, means providing equality, equity, and opportunity for all children.

The Rev. Odell Cleveland, president of Cal-Tee Solutions, said families should have the ability to pursue choice in education, but all too often a lack of transportation options makes it difficult to pursue different educational opportunities.

"Transportation will allow them to have access to exercise their choices," Cleveland said.

Addul Ali, a business owner and charter school advocate in Cabarrus County, said he would take what Cleveland said a step further.

"I'd say without transportation they don't have a choice," Ali said.

Ali said children are successful when they are able to go to a school that meets their needs. H.B. 199 will help families accomplish this goal.

Sebastian King, board member at Next Generation Academy; Mary Catherine Sauer, board chair of Revolution Charter School; the Rev. Leon Threatt, pastor at Victory Christian Assembly; the Rev. Kevrick McKain, vice president of Douglass Leadership Institute; Rhonda Dillingham, executive director of the N.C. Association for Public Charter Schools; Shamike Bethea, a representative with the Frederick

Douglass Foundation of N.C.; and Clarence Henderson, president of the Frederick Douglass Foundation of N.C. and civil rights pioneer, all spoke out for H.B. 199.

The House Education Committee approved H.B. 199 on April 9. Hardister said the bill has bipartisan support, and only two committee members voted against it. H.B. 199 heads to the House Appropriations Committee on Education.

Editor's note: A previous version of this story incorrectly stated Addul Ali is from Davidson County. He works out of Cabarrus County. We regret the error.

Woolworth's Protester Shares Views in Pinehurst Speech

By JAYMIE BAXLEY • jaymie@thepilot.com

Jan 17, 2020 Updated Jan 17, 2020

Sixty years ago, Clarence Henderson was among the 20 demonstrators who participated in the second day of sit-ins at a racially segregated department store in Greensboro.

Orchestrated by four students at North Carolina A&T State University, the sit-ins were a watershed for the Civil Rights movement. Addressing a crowd of nearly 250 people Thursday at The Fair Barn in Pinehurst, Henderson said the peaceful protest was a "shot heard around the world."

"I was all of 18 years of age, and my parents knew about it after the fact," he recalled of joining the lunch counter sit-in, adding that he chose to participate "so all could eat in the same place."

Henderson said he was not publicly recognized for his role in the demonstration until the early 2000s, when a newspaper misidentified him in the caption for a photograph made at the Woolworth store where the sit-ins took place.

"They had the wrong name on the picture," Henderson said. "I never murmured or complained, because I knew that I was there."

Thursday's event was organized by the Moore County GOP, and the audience included several rivals in the upcoming Republican primary elections. Henderson, who has delivered multiple invocations for President Donald Trump and Vice President Mike Pence, said he has received criticism for his support of the administration.

The septuagenarian did not mince words during his 40-minute presentation. He derided the Black Lives Matter movement, LGBTQ people, the news media, the public education system, climate change activists, Trump's impeachment trial and socialism, which he said "can in a way be worse than segregation."

"They put you in classes," he said. "And whatever class you're in, that's where you remain."

During his wide-ranging address, Henderson praised law enforcers, military personnel and "free-market capitalism." He said his father, a sharecropper-turned-mechanic with a "third-grade education," was his hero.

"When he left the farm, he never worked for anybody but himself," Henderson said. "I have seen times when the dealerships in Greensboro would bring cars to him that their guys couldn't fix, and he never took one class."

An army veteran, Henderson served as chairman of the North Carolina Martin Luther King, Jr. Commission under former Gov. Pat McCrory. Henderson's address included several references to the Civil Rights icon, whose life will be celebrated across the U.S. on Monday.

Clarence Henderson: President Donald Trump Has Ended the Era of Broken Promises by Delivering Real Results for African Americans

Feb 9, 2020

Joseph Rodriguez/News & Record

Donald Trump has done more to empower African Americans than any U.S. president since Abraham Lincoln — and he's just getting started.

Since February is Black History Month, now is an excellent time to reflect on the incredible progress African Americans have made over the past three years.

Before Trump, the black community endured decades of broken promises from the political establishment in Washington. For years, liberal politicians have vowed to tackle the sky-high black unemployment rate and create jobs for African Americans. They pledged to implement policies that would boost our income, insisting that poverty can be cured with welfare.

Yet, after winning our votes, Democratic politicians — including President Barack Obama — either ignored the needs of African Americans or demonstrated the futility of their discredited socialist policies. Much like the tax rate, the black unemployment rate remained high throughout the Obama years, contributing to widespread suffering among millions of African Americans. Instead of collecting higher paychecks, more and more black families were forced to rely on food stamps — depriving them of the dignity that comes with being able to provide for one's own family.

When Trump won the 2016 election, I kept my expectations in check regarding how much he could do for African Americans during his first term, given that his policies would have to make it through Congress. Remarkably, however, Trump only needed three years to create the best economy for African Americans in U.S. history.

Thanks to Trump's economic reforms, such as targeted deregulation and middle-class tax cuts, the black unemployment rate dropped to an all-time low of 5.4% in August 2019, and has hovered below 6% ever since. Notably, the jobless rate among African Americans was a whopping 7.5% when Obama left office — a contrast that highlights the transformative impact that Trump's policies have had for black Americans.

Black North Carolinians are at the forefront of this economic resurgence. As a result, our brothers and sisters whose grandparents and great-grandparents moved to cities in the North in search of jobs are now returning to North Carolina as Democratic mismanagement ravages the inner cities.

Cutting taxes and eliminating job-killing regulations isn't all this president has done for African Americans, though. The White House Opportunity Zone project, for instance, will promote massive economic investment in the very communities that were abandoned for so long by establishment politicians.

Trump also managed to rally bipartisan support for one of the most extensive criminal justice reform efforts in our country's history, ending discriminatory sentencing policies and creating new pathways for former inmates to lead productive, crime-free lives after they finish paying their debt to society.

All of these commonsense policies and reforms could have been instituted long before Trump ran for office — but the political establishment was more concerned with winning elections than delivering results. Former NFL player Jack Brewer — who once was a fundraiser for Obama — said it best when he recently called out the Democrats for paying "lip service" to African American voters.

"There is an awakening going on right now in the country," Brewer said last month. "I'm going to take the guy who's actually putting in the policies that are going to make life better for my young black son and my young black daughter, versus somebody who gives me lip service — like, unfortunately, the Democrats have done for our community for years."

This Black History Month, we should all celebrate everything that Trump has done for African Americans over the past three years, and eagerly anticipate the gains that are in store over the next five years. For the first time in living memory, this country has a president who is delivering on his promises to black voters — and that's why we must do everything in our power to ensure that Donald Trump gets four more years in the White House.

President Trump Speaks At "Salute To America" Event

Jul 4, 2019

President Trump says America is stronger now than it has ever been before. Trump is spoke at a "Salute To America" event in front of the Lincoln Memorial in Washington, DC. Trump remarked that it's an occasion to come together as one nation to celebrate America's history and people, as well as its heroes in the military. He invoked the memory of General George Washington, who led the Continental Army in a campaign against British forces in the Revolutionary War. Trump said Washington's spirit lives on in every American. He also highlighted the legacy of American inventors Thomas Edison, Alexander Graham Bell, and the Wright Brothers. He remarked that for Americans, nothing is impossible.

President Trump paid tribute to several important Americans, both present and past. He invoked abolitionists Harriet Tubman and Frederick Douglass, aviator Amelia Earhart, senator and astronaut John Glenn and civil rights icon Jackie Robinson. He also highlighted civil rights protester Clarence Henderson, who was present at today's event. Henderson took part in the famous sit-in at a Woolworth lunch counter in Greensboro, North Carolina, in 1960.

Trump then turned his attention to each branch of the military, highlighting the important roles each play. After each mention of a branch, there was a flyover of military aircraft.

Two Activists: Conservatives Are Not Doing Enough to Reach Black Voters

April 21, 2020 by Andy Jackson

- **About 90 percent of African Americans consistently vote Democratic**
- **If Republicans could garner just 14-16 percent of their vote, it would be "game over"**
- **Two activists share their thoughts on how the GOP could improve outreach to the African American community**

President Trump, through both his actions and words, is clearly seeking to reach out to African Americans ahead of the 2020 general election.

The insistence and persistence of his effort has caused observers to take Trump's outreach seriously. Sen. Tim Scott (R-SC), the first African American Senator from the South since Reconstruction, said that Trump could increase his share of the black vote from roughly eight percent in 2016 to 14-16 percent this year, adding that it would be "game over if we get 14 percent."

Progressive activist and CNN regular Van Jones takes this potential swing seriously and says that Democrats need to "wake up" to the fact that "what he was saying to African-Americans can be effective" in gaining black votes.

However, Trump and other Republicans face serious headwinds in their efforts to woo black voters; about ninety percent of African Americans vote Democratic in most elections. For example, according to an exit poll by CNN in 2016, Republican candidates in

North Carolina only earned eight percent of the black vote for president, twelve percent for governor, and nine percent for senator.

To gain a better understanding of that dynamic, I spoke separately with two activists who are seeking to get black conservatives and moderates to vote in a way that is consistent with their beliefs: Clarence Henderson, President of the Frederick Douglass Foundation of North Carolina, and Danielle Robinson, a founding member of BLEXIT North Carolina.

Issues are not why 90 percent of African Americans vote Democratic

Both Henderson and Robinson see a disconnect between the voting habits of many African Americans and where they stand on issues. Robinson finds that disconnect in her work:

Why do we vote consistently against our values? Many blacks are conservative and many blacks are faithful traditional Christians. We traditionally engage in small business and see government aid as temporary. I am not against social service; there was a time when I needed support. But I am against the attitude that blacks need the government, or that we want to trust the government with everything.

Henderson, a long-time civil rights activist who participated in the famous 1960 Greensboro Woolworth lunch counter sit-in, sounded a similar theme, saying "the Great Society [social welfare programs developed during Lyndon Johnson's presidency] did damage to black families." He also noted strong support among African Americans for school choice as a way for children to escape failing schools: "kids are being held captive within the public schools," Henderson said. However, it may be difficult for Republicans to significantly increase their support among black voters, even those who are conservative on most issues. That is due to what political scientists Ismail K. White and Cheryl N. Laird call "radicalized social constraint," a phenomenon which causes many blacks who are conservative on most issues to nevertheless vote Democratic:

[A] significant minority of African Americans – nearly a third, White and Laird report – consider themselves conservative and share at least some Republican economic and social positions. It is on this segment of the black electorate that intragroup social pressure primarily operates, causing many to back Democrats, the authors argue.

So, perhaps it is social pressure, not issues, that is the main barrier to conservatives making gains among moderate and conservative black voters.

What Republicans need to do: persistent outreach

So how can conservative candidates break through that barrier?

Both Henderson and Robinson insist that the Republican Party cannot gain support from black voters without a persistent and concerted effort to show how the Republican Party benefits them and aligns with their values. Robinson believes that the party has been blind to the potential of attracting more black voters:

[The GOP] has mistakenly believed that the black vote cannot be won. That it is a done deal and with no vehicle to reach us, they simply have not been able to do so.

Henderson takes a similar view, saying that the Republican Party "is not effectively communicating" with black voters and that they "need to share with blacks what the GOP has accomplished and how that benefits blacks," adding:

Republicans have been unable to frame the conversation based on values and policies, such as school choice, abortion, and creating business opportunities, rather than identity. They need to educate on what the party represents.

For Henderson, that means keeping a presence among black voters: "Don't just come to black churches at election time." One way he suggests making a more enduring presence is for the party and Republican campaigns to hire more African Americans. This creates a bit of a catch-22 since the current weakness the Republican Party has among black voters means that there is a small potential pool of qualified black campaign workers available for Republicans to hire. Robinson sees that dilemma but addresses it in a different way:

Blexit is not a feeder group to the GOP. However, we are providing information to our community about the other side and what conservative values really mean. That's where we increase the quality of black civic engagement, by providing the information they need to vote their values.

Perhaps Lt. Gov. Dan Forests' campaign for governor will be a test case. Henderson has been helping Forest reach out to members of the black community and sees him engaging with black pastors and others on issues that are important to them. If Forest can manage to get that "game over" 14 percent of the black vote, other conservatives will seek to emulate that success so that the two parties will genuinely compete for black votes.

What you can do

To find out more about the organizations mentioned in this article, contact the Frederick Douglas Foundation of North Carolina and Blexit North Carolina.

OPINION

Published June 19, 2020

CLARENCE HENDERSON: GEORGE FLOYD PROTESTS — WHAT I LEARNED DURING LUNCH COUNTER SIT-INS IN 1960

By Clarence Henderson | **Fox News**

"Clarence, what can we do to make things better?"

I've heard that question countless times in the last few weeks, as the senseless murders of Ahmaud Arbery, Breonna Taylor and George Floyd flooded the headlines, filling us all with horror and grief. Many decent Americans want to do something to demonstrate solidarity with the black community and work to end racial injustice. But what?

I have been in the civil rights fight for a very long time. When I was 8 or 9 years old, I was riding my bicycle down a sidewalk, when I saw a white man walking toward me. I moved all the way over to get out of his way, and he turned, walked right to where I was, and knocked me off my bicycle.

Growing up, I knew that the world was full of white people who thought they could treat me any way they wanted and get away with it.

For me, the civil rights movement was always rooted in morality. Since my involvement in the Greensboro Woolworth's lunch counter sit-it in 1960, my goal was to ensure that blacks were treated with the respect and dignity that all Americans deserve under the law.

That dignity doesn't come from the law; it comes from God. Good law recognizes what God has already said: that we all bear His image and deserve to be respected.

Every black person I grew up with knew we had to be better — nearly perfect, in fact — to hope to get the treatment and benefit of the doubt that seemed to be automatically afforded to whites. This is, and has always been, fundamentally wrong and unfair.

We should never deceive ourselves to think we can ever sufficiently "earn" the respect of the worst racists: that man who knocked me off my bike wouldn't have cared if I was a straight A student or an usher in my church. But at the same time, we cannot let that unfairness lure us into self-destructive behavior, just to prove a point.

There have always been different models for black Americans to work for progress and equality. Without delving into all the details, these models have fallen into two major categories: those who believe that America was founded on good principles that it has often failed to put into practice, and those who believe that America is evil at its root and must be destroyed and replaced.

Those in the first category — like Martin Luther King, Jr. and Frederick Douglass — believe that America is in a continual process of reformation, striving to live up to our best ideals. Those in the second want to fundamentally remake America as an entirely different kind of country.

I am a reformer who affirms America and wants to make it better, and I work with and support organizations like the Frederick Douglass Foundation that believe the same. While I believe — like all decent people — that black lives absolutely do matter, I am concerned that the policy goals of the official BLM organization fall more into the second category. FDF and I believe that the traditional family — supported, not disrupted, by extended kin — is the ideal environment to raise children and the foundation for all success, including upward mobility. We work to strengthen families by supporting marriage and parental rights and offering training and resources for community leaders.

I am a reformer who affirms America and wants to make it better, and I work with and support organizations like the Frederick Douglass Foundation that believe the same.

We also believe in reforming the existing system of criminal justice through reducing overcriminalization at every level, working to prevent criminality and recidivism, advocating for deescalation training for all police departments and working toward improving community-police relations wherever needed.

But perhaps our most substantive difference with BLM is that we believe that the free exchange of goods and services creates the greatest economic opportunity for all people regardless of race or background.

We believe in the right to own property, the right to own one's own labor, and the right to make a living legally and ethically.

We believe in a free market of education, where all parents can choose what is best for their children from a variety of options.

We do not support policies that infringe on these rights.

And most of all, we believe that the best way to lift people out of poverty is to create a society where all can prosper together.

First Woman Freed by Criminal Justice Reform Thanks Donald Trump at Black History Month Reception

CHARLIE SPIERING
21 Feb 2019

The first woman freed as the result of Donald Trump's criminal reform bill joined him at the White House on Thursday during a reception for Black History Month.

Catherine Toney, joined by her daughter and granddaughter, spoke to the group, thanking the president for signing the criminal justice reform bill that helped her win her freedom.

"If it wasn't for them, I wouldn't be standing up here today," she said, noting that she was incarcerated for sixteen years before she was freed.

Trump was greeted with cheers as he took the podium at the reception as several attendees wearing Make America Great Again campaign hats chanted "Trump! Trump! Trump!"

The president praised African-Americans who championed civil rights and freedom in the United States.

"Today we thank God for all the blessings that the African-American community continues to give our nation and we pledge our resolve to expand opportunity for Americans of every race, color, and creed," he said.

Trump noted that heightened sentencing rules disproportionally affected the African-American community, which was why he signed the First STEP Act. "Nobody thought we could get this done, we worked with conserva-tives and liberals, and those in the middle, we worked with a lot of people and we got this done," Trump said.

He credited his son-in-law Jared Kushner for working to get the bill passed.

During the reception, one civil rights activist took the podium to thank Trump for building a wall.

"You know Nehemiah was told by God to build a wall and that's what you're doing. Amen," Civil rights activist Clarence Henderson of the Fredrick Douglass Foundation said during the president's remarks at the reception.

Civil rights leader Bob Woodson also thanked the president for shaking up the establishment.

"I just want to thank God and President Trump for turning over the tables in the temples and attacking the status quo that is hostile to the interests of poor people," Woodson said, noting that all the poor needed was the opportunity to achieve greatness.

HENDERSON: THE LEGACY OF DR. MARTIN LUTHER KING JR.

January 16, 2022 Clarence Henderson Article, Opinion

In this Tuesday, Sept. 20, 2016, image made from video, Clarence Henderson, a participant in the Feb. 1, 1960, sit-in at a Greensboro, N.C., Woolworth lunch counter, speaks at a campaign event in High Point, N.C., in support of Republican presidential candidate Donald Trump. Henderson has been criticized for his stance, with many taking to Twitter to accuse him of abandoning the principles he fought so hard for more than half a century ago. (AP Photo/Alex Sanz)

As we celebrate the life and legacy of Dr. Martin Luther King Jr. let us remember who he was and what he represented. He was a great civil rights leader advocating for equality. He believed that people should be judged by the content of their character rather than the color of their skin.

This idea united Americans around the self-evident truths that underpin this nation and it is the same idea that caused the emergence of the Woolworth Sit-in that I participated in. Why were both of these necessary? If you look at American history with open eyes, the reason is quite obvious.

When we examine the political parties in our country it is apparent that the Democratic Party was at the forefront of racism in America. Unfortunately, half a century later, they still are. Today Democrats want to make race a central factor in how we treat each other as Americans. They want to divide us based on our identities, not unite us around our common values.

What do Democrats hope to achieve by promoting this division?

It certainly isn't Dr. King's dream they strive for.

Dr. King fought for equality under the law and the moral precept of judging individuals by their character and actions, not the pigment of their skin. It's no secret that today's Democrat Party and the modern Woke movement that fuels them do not believe in these principles. In fact, they openly oppose them. They promote disdain for our fellow Americans based on race, or religion, or even on vaccination status.

The language the Democrats speak today – such as critical race theory (CRT), social justice, cancel culture and equity – is used to keep the black community with the mindset that we are victims or survivors when we are neither. We are overcomers, having overcome slavery as well as Jim Crow.

They are currently using CRT as a way to exploit our educational systems to teach the black community to judge the white community by the color of their skin rather than the content of their character. They are promoting the sin of racism we fought so hard to overcome, and brazenly claiming the moral high ground while doing so.

This is causing a great divide in America when we should be living according to the words of Dr. King, "Unless we learn to live together as brothers, we will perish together as fools."

This Martin Luther King Jr. Day, as we see his dream slipping away – being torn away – we Americans must reach deep to find the courage that Dr. King demonstrated. We must call upon this courage to revitalize his dream – the American Dream – for a world in which we can live together as brothers and sisters, as Americans.

A world in which we are judged by our merit, where the principle of equality under the law and the God-given rights of man reign supreme over sinister calls for 'equity' and radical justice.

In 2022, we must remember the true legacy of Dr. King and find the courage to reject any movement or government that would divide us in the name of racism.

Civil Rights Hero Clarence Henderson: The future is bright for Black North Carolinians, Just Not With 'Do Nothing Democrats'

BY

FIRSTINFREEDOMDAILY

November 25, 2019

(Clarence Henderson is a civil rights activist and recipient of the 40th Anniversary Sit-In Participant Award. He also serves as a member of the Black Voices for Trump coalition advisory board. He writes below on a bright future, lest North Carolinians and Americans let Democrats dim it.)

Since President Trump took office, North Carolina has prospered. His pro-growth economic agenda and focus on creating opportunities for African Americans has led to a bright future for the Tar Heel State.

In 2018, North Carolina was voted the best state in which to do business for the second year in a row. Business investment continues to pour into the state, leading to rapid job creation and robust wage growth — between July 2018 and July 2019 alone, North Carolina created more than 75,000 new jobs thanks to President Trump.

Wage growth has also increased evenly across different pay grades, instead of being concentrated among white collar professionals as it has in the past. President Trump's economy is creating the high-paying blue collar jobs that are essential to upward mobility, and empowering the formerly-forgotten men and women who had been neglected by do-nothing Democrats. African Americans, in particular, are making unprecedented gains in the Trump economy.

Black unemployment is at an all-time low, and the unemployment gap between white and black Americans is smaller than it has ever been. Since President Trump took office, total African American employment has increased by more than one million new jobs. President Trump is proving Frederick Douglass correct: we don't need the Democrats or their policies to take care of us, we just need to be left alone and given the opportunity to pursue our own interests.

The President has also taken innovative steps to solve the problem of underinvestment and economic stagnation in low-income communi-ties. The "Opportunity Zones" initiative created by the President's tax cut law will drive a projected $100 billion worth of new investment to economically distressed neighborhoods. There are 252 officially-designated Opportunity Zones in North Carolina alone, including in many predominantly-black communities.

These investments will create new manufacturing, technology, and retail establishments within those communities, providing African Americans living in Opportunity Zones with real opportunities to build generational wealth, instead of perpetuating a state of dependence.

Do-nothing Democrats want to erase these gains and advance a big-government socialist agenda. They're not interested in treating blacks as independent Americans capable of standing on our own two feet. That's the exact opposite of what I and so many others fought for as part of the Civil Rights movement. We want equality under the law and the chance to provide for our families, not the insulting paternal-ism of disingenuous liberals.

African Americans are prospering thanks to President Trump's economic policies. That may not be a big deal to elitist Democrats, who would gladly sacrifice our well-being in pursuit of their own political ambitions, but it means a lot to black people!

That's why I am excited to join Black Voices for Trump to help spread that message of "Promises Made, Promises Kept" throughout the African American community. The progress we've made under President Trump has been incredible, and there's a lot more prosperity yet to come over the next five years.

Clarence Henderson is a civil rights activist and recipient of the 40th Anniversary Sit-In Participant Award. He also serves as a member of the Black Voices for Trump coalition advisory board.

[EXCLUSIVE OP-ED] CLARENCE HENDERSON: Biden is as good at debating as he is bad at governing

BY

FIRSTINFREEDOMDAILY

-

September 28, 2020

(Clarence Henderson is a civil rights activist and recipient of the 40th Anniversary Sit-In Participant Award. A North Carolina native, he also serves as a member of the Black Voices for Trump coalition advisory board.)

Voters should expect to see a competent performance by Joe Biden on the debate stage, but don't let his polished rhetoric mask his tarnished record.

Biden is a career politician who has spent nearly half a century in Washington, D.C. During that time, he has run for president three times and vice president twice, giving him abundant experience in nationally-televised debates. He knows how to deliver canned talking points and deflect tough questions with folksy platitudes. He'll undoubtedly rely on those skills when he faces off against President Trump, but nothing he says on the debate stage can change the fact that his record is one of consistent failure on every major challenge our country has faced.

In the 1970s, he strongly opposed busing as a means of integrating public schools, siding with Southern segregationists whom he still recalls fondly. Senator Kamala Harris forcefully called him out on this during one of the Democratic primary debates, but Biden managed to blunt the attack with a non-answer. The spat had so little effect on Biden that he later chose Harris as his running mate.

In the 1980s, Biden staked out a position as a "tough-on-crime" politician, boasting of his "lock the S.O.B.'s up" philosophy while crafting policies that resulted in the mass incarceration of Black Americans for non-violent crimes. When this became a liability in the current election cycle, however, he shamelessly flip-flopped and pretended to be a compassionate supporter of criminal justice reform.

In the 1990s and 2000s, Biden took his goofy approach to governing global, spearheading disastrous policies such as NAFTA that sacrificed the interests of American workers to foreign competitors. He was also instrumental in enabling China to rip our country off in historic fashion.

Americans are well aware that China is a dangerous rival. Even before the communist regime's deadly mishandling of the coronavirus outbreak that began in Wuhan, China, we suffered the loss of millions of jobs due to China's unfair and illegal trade practices. China's rise to become the world's second-largest economy wouldn't have been possible without help from establishment politicians in America such as Joe Biden, though.

Biden supported granting China "most favored nation" trading status, paving the way for its eventual entrance into the World Trading Organization (WTO), a move that caused extensive and lasting damage to blue collar industries in North Carolina and other states. Between 2001 and 2008, an estimated 80,000 North

Carolinians lost their livelihoods to China, thanks in large part to the policies Biden helped to put in place. Now, though, Biden has the audacity to fraudulently portray himself as a China hawk — a contortion he can only hope to pull off through brazen gaslighting. He demonstrated during the primaries that he's perfectly comfortable contradicting himself on the debate stage, relying on folksiness to charm uninformed voters into taking him at his word even when it runs contrary to his previous actions.

Joe Biden can debate blindfolded with his hands behind his back and still avoid taking any mortal political blows. But there is nothing he can do to change the fact that he has spent nearly half a century consistently failing the American people on every meaningful issue, and we shouldn't let him distract us from that atrocious record.

HENDERSON: THE LEGACY OF DR. MARTIN LUTHER KING JR.

January 16, 2022 Clarence Henderson Article, Opinion

As we celebrate the life and legacy of Dr. Martin Luther King Jr. let us remember who he was and what he represented. He was a great civil rights leader advocating for equality. He believed that people should be judged by the content of their character rather than the color of their skin.

This idea united Americans around the self-evident truths that underpin this nation and it is the same idea that caused the emergence of the Woolworth Sit-in that I participated in. Why were both of these necessary? If you look at American history with open eyes, the reason is quite obvious.

When we examine the political parties in our country it is apparent that the Democratic Party was at the forefront of racism in America. Unfortunately, half a century later, they still are. Today Democrats want to make race a central factor in how we treat each other as Americans. They want to divide us based on our identities, not unite us around our common values.

What do Democrats hope to achieve by promoting this division?

It certainly isn't Dr. King's dream they strive for.

Dr. King fought for equality under the law and the moral precept of judging individuals by their character and actions, not the pigment of their skin. It's no secret that today's Democrat Party and the modern Woke movement that fuels them do not believe in these principles. In fact, they openly oppose them. They promote disdain for our fellow Americans based on race, or religion, or even on vaccination status.

The language the Democrats speak today – such as critical race theory (CRT), social justice, cancel culture and equity – is used to keep the black community with the mindset that we are victims or survivors when we are neither. We are overcomers, having overcome slavery as well as Jim Crow.

They are currently using CRT as a way to exploit our educational systems to teach the black community to judge the white community by the color of their skin rather than the content of their character. They are promoting the sin of racism we fought so hard to overcome, and brazenly claiming the moral high ground while doing so.

This is causing a great divide in America when we should be living according to the words of Dr. King, "Unless we learn to live together as brothers, we will perish together as fools."

This Martin Luther King Jr. Day, as we see his dream slipping away – being torn away – we Americans must reach deep to find the courage that Dr. King demonstrated. We must call upon this courage to revitalize his dream – the American Dream – for a world in which we can live together as brothers and sisters, as Americans. A world in which we are judged by our merit, where the principle of equality under the law and the God-given rights of man reign supreme over sinister calls for 'equity' and radical justice.

In 2022, we must remember the true legacy of Dr. King and find the courage to reject any movement or government that would divide us in the name of racism.

CP VOICES | TUESDAY, FEBRUARY 23, 2021

Liberal hypocrisy on full display with racist cartoon

By Timothy Head and Clarence Henderson, Op-ed Contributors | Tuesday, February 23, 2021

The media has long given Democrats and liberals a free pass to act with impunity. Honest mistakes, distasteful remarks, or even just unpopular opinions can easily ruin any Republican's reputation, and possibly even their career. But outright slander or truly unconscionable behavior by Democrats is met with a shrug.

The recent actions by North Carolina's WRAL provide a case in point. In response to a perfectly civil and reasonable debate about new stan-dards for the state's public school curriculum, WRAL published an editorial cartoon depicting Lieutenant Governor Mark Robinson as a member of the KKK. And so far, no one in the mainstream media seems to care.

Now, there's a lot that's objectively wrong with this kind of vicious misrepresentation of a politician's personal character and political views. Anyone would have a right to be offended by this image, especially in today's environment when even the most groundless accusations of racism can generate a social media firestorm.

But Lt. Governor Mark Robinson has the right to be positively incensed, because he is the first ever Black Republican to hold the position of Lt. Governor in North Carolina. And instead of being celebrated for the diversity he brings to the GOP and to North Carolina, he is being cast as an anti-Black, racist villain.

We can only imagine the anger that Lt. Governor Robinson must feel. As a Black American, the scourge of the KKK's racism and hatred must weigh heavily on his heart and mind. It's a brutal, unconscionable slap in the face for anyone in the media to portray him as aligned with the goals, mission, values or history of the KKK.

Normally, events and offenses that truly pale in comparison to this are more than enough to unleash hours, if not days, of mainstream media coverage. Who remembers when we were subjected to unending media commentary about racism in NASCAR after a completely normal garage pull rope was photographed hanging in a Talladega garage? And who can forget that for the last four years, the media has jumped on every single thing that President Trump has said, using every speech he has made to argue that he was a racist or a white supremacist?

Yet now, when an editorial cartoon is, *in fact,* racist in its attack on a Black American, the media doesn't care. After Lt. Governor Robinson gave a press conference asking for answers about the racist cartoon, the opinion editor for Capitol Broadcasting – owner of WRAL – released a lackluster and unapologetic statement claiming the cartoon was "creative and provocative" and just using "hyperbole and satire."

The hypocrisy is truly dumbfounding. You can't call racism "creative and provocative" just when liberals do it. If racism means anything at all, then it shouldn't matter where it comes from or who it's directed at. But WRAL's editorial cartoon shows quite clearly that unless racism is politically useful to the left's ongoing campaign to slander conservatives, it goes unnoticed, unacknowledged and swept under the rug. Liberals care more about weaponizing racism and whipping up moral fervor to bully their opponents than they actually care about Black Americans.

And make no mistake about it: we all know what would have happened if the cartoonist were Republican and the target of the cartoon were a Black Democrat. Let us run through the likeliest scenario for you. The cartoonist would be immediately fired. After days of mounting social media anger, WRAL would issue a heartfelt apology. The apology would have little effect. There would be protests in the streets. And for weeks, every mainstream media article would reference the incident as yet another sign that the Republican Party is full of racist, ignorant hatemongers.

It's appalling that we live in a cultural and political environment where the game is so blatantly rigged against conservatives. If it wasn't already obvious, the mainstream media controls what "counts" as racism and what doesn't. With that kind of power, why should we ever expect the media to be honest and fair again?

Timothy Head is the executive director of the Faith and Freedom Coalition. Clarence Henderson is the President of Frederick Douglass Foundation of North Carolina.

The North State Journal

HENDERSON: Are N.C. Republicans bad for Black Families?

July 19, 2017 admin Opinion

North Carolina Senate President Pro Tempore Phil Berger

In a recent op-ed in another newspaper ("The NC GOP have failed to address racial issues in the state," June 29) UNC Chapel Hill professor Gene Nichol displays the usual condescending hysteria of white elites who claim to care deeply about African Americans. He portrays the entire black citizenry of North Carolina as impoverished, poorly educated serfs being viciously subjected to "systemic racial subordination" by their evil Republican overlords. In the same breath, Nichol lauds Rev. William Barber — a bombastic advocate for public school monopolies, coercive wealth redistribution and abortion on demand — as "the nation's paramount rising civil rights leader." Like so many whites in positions of power, Nichol assumes that blacks — unlike whites — are unable to hold diverse opinions about these controversial issues. I am a lifelong resident of North Carolina who survived the "terror-enforced Jim Crow" that Nichol speculates Republicans might not remember, and I participated in the 1960 Woolworth sit-in in Greensboro. (I also remember such atrocities occurred under Democratic rule in the statehouse and governorship, a fact Nichol conveniently forgets to mention.) While I share Nichol's concern for our most vulnerable citizens, I do not share his conviction that the North Carolina Republican Party is the villain in this story. In fact, I think several Republican policies hold the key for the improvement of black lives in our state and our nation as a whole. Let's take one of Nichol's concerns that I share: "Black children attend high-poverty, troubled schools very, very disproportionately." We are to believe that Republicans have failed to respond to this tragic reality when in fact it is North Carolina Republicans who have been fighting tirelessly for school choice. Only the legislative freedom for all parents — regardless of income — to choose the school their children attend will liberate them from be-ing forced to attend failing public schools simply because such schools serve the neighborhoods where their parents can afford a home. Yet such measures have been consistently opposed by Democrats and men like Barber, the "hero" Nichol exalts. Nichol mourns that "Almost 40 percent of black kids are poor, compared to 12 percent of white ones." True enough. Yet he fails to note that black children with married parents fare almost identically to white children. In 2009, 40.6 percent of single-parent families with children in North Carolina lived in poverty, while only 7.2 percent of married couples with children were poor. Seventy-two percent of black children in North Carolina are born to single mothers, compared to 26.5 percent of white children. The best weapon against black child poverty in North Carolina is strong black marriages. The issues Nichol raises around criminal justice reform are very complicated, and I cannot do them full justice in this short response. But it is worth pointing out that a third of the murderers who have used The Racial Justice Act to challenge the death penalty were white. Because the law is so ambiguously written, white men, convicted by white juries, have been able to logjam the justice system by arguing that they were victims of discrimination, based on minute differences between themselves and their jurors. So clearly the "systemic racial subordination" Nichol feels Republicans promote is a little more complicated than he is letting on. Republicans gained control of both houses of the North Carolina legislature in 2010 for the first time since 1896. Would Nichol really have us believe that life for blacks in North Carolina was a blissful paradise before the evil Republicans began oppressing them?

Or perhaps he feels we would be better off back in the hands of the party that subjected us to Jim Crow? Democrats have long been professionals at rehearsing grievances and acting like they care.

The black citizens of North Carolina don't need the pity of academics. They need policy changes that will strengthen black marriages and families, encourage economic growth, and allow them to choose the schools their children attend.

Clarence Henderson is chairman of the N.C. Martin Luther King, Jr. Commission, president of the Frederick Douglass Foundation of North Carolina, and a Republican. He lives in High Point.

— OPINION —

MENKEN/HENDERSON: Donald Trump Is Healing The Country

By Yaakov Menken

﹡

May 28, 2019 DailyWire.com

﹡

From the moment President Donald Trump launched his run for office in 2016, the media and the Left have claimed that he has used racially-charged language and exacerbated ethnic tensions in this country. A pair of sociologists at the University of Pennsylvania, Daniel Hopkins and Samantha Washington, recently set out to measure the result of what they described as President Trump's "explicit, negative rhetoric targeting ethnic/racial minorities."

What they discovered was, to them, astounding. Though they expected racism to be flourishing under Trump, "white Americans' expressed anti-black and anti-Hispanic prejudice declined after the 2016 campaign and election" [emphasis theirs]. After carefully studying the evidence proving the media's claims to be false, they came to the sort of truly learned conclusion only possible in the ivory towers of academia: This demonstrated a "thermostatic response," in which people move in the opposite direction from their leaders.

The possibility that their underlying assumption might be as faulty as their hypothesis never seemed to cross their minds.

Writing in the Spectator, Ross Clark offered a second option: "[I]t was the sight of a mixed race man in the White House who brought out in the inner racist in Americans who are inclined towards those feelings, while the reassuring sight of a white man back in the Oval Office has calmed them down."

So while the professors apparently believe that electing David Duke would do still better things for race relations in America, Clark offers the possibility that any old white guy would do just fine. Neither of these options should strike us as reassuring. Fortunately, there is reason to believe that both of them are wrong.

Yes, the media has insisted that Trump is a racist, just as the media told us that John McCain and Mitt Romney were racists before Trump. But Americans have discerned that it simply isn't true. Trump may be politically incorrect and imprecise with his language, but he is neither a racist nor an anti-Semite. Actually, it is just the opposite — he enacts policies to equally benefit all Americans, and appears to take special pleasure celebrating minority achievement.

Back in 2008, many who voted for McCain felt great pride in a country that instead elected Barack Obama less than two generations removed from the end of racist laws designed to systemically oppress African-Americans. And then, sadly, President Obama undid much of the progress made via his election.

It was not Obama's ethnicity, but his actions that triggered what Clark describes as "a more fractious period in race relations." Obama repeatedly took positions in racially-charged disputes that exacerbated tensions rather than reducing them. He claimed that police "acted stupidly" in arresting a professor who became disorderly when asked for identification, described a simple defensive shooting as the result of a "broken and racially biased system," and famously said that "if I had a son, he would look like Trayvon [Martin]." That last anecdote was surely unrelated to Trayvon Martin's previous history or the circumstances under which he was shot. Obama claimed kinship based upon shared race and upon no other factor.

Trump has never operated that way, but the media still diligently tries to paint him that way. The vast majority of the president's supporters are not racists, but are instead people who see in him none of the things that the media claim embody him.

They know that the president neither mocked a reporter's disability nor called neo-Nazis "fine people." He never envisioned a "Muslim ban" — only an eminently reasonable travel ban from countries that are hotbeds of radical Islamic terrorism. He never said "Mexicans" are rapists, but accused Mexico of "sending people that have lots of problems" to the U.S. These false claims of bias provide much of the impetus behind the president's frequent derision of "fake news."

In reality, the president has allocated more money to historically black colleges and universities (HBCUs) than any predecessor — including Obama — and signed a crucial executive order directing funds to HBCUs just six weeks into his presidency. And he has continually celebrated the decline in black unemployment, which is now at its lowest in history.

No one would describe the man responsible for integrating Palm Beach country clubs as a racist were it not for cynical, partisan considerations. Perhaps racism in America is not declining, despite the man in the White House, but thanks in part to his insistence upon ensuring that every American has a chance to pursue the American dream.

Unquestionably, and unlike the anti-black and anti-Hispanic prejudice measured in the survey, there is more anti-Semitism in America than there was two years ago. But President Trump is not to blame for that, either. Anti-Semites hate Trump's affinity for Jews, and this is as true for leftist anti-Semites as it is for the synagogue shooters of both Pittsburgh and Poway.

Besides his great friendship towards Israel, three of the President's clos-est advisors for decades have been observant, Orthodox Jews. One is his son-in-law, father of the president's observant Jewish grandchil-dren. Rabbi Yisroel Goldstein, wounded at his synagogue in Poway, called Trump 'a mensch par excellence' after their interactions, and few in the Orthodox community were surprised.

Why, then, is anti-Semitism increasing? In September of last year, Lord Rabbi Jonathan Sacks addressed his peers and spoke about this same topic in England. He said this:

Anti-Semitism, or any hate, become dangerous when three things happen. First: When it moves from the fringes of politics to a mainstream party and its leadership. Second: When the party sees that its popularity with the general public is not harmed thereby. And three: When those who stand up and protest are vilified and abused for doing so. All three factors exist in Britain now.

Lord Rabbi Sacks could not have known how prescient this warning would also prove to be in America. Members of Congress elected afterward have espoused anti-Semitic views of a kind familiar to Jews throughout history, but foreign to modern America and American values. Leading members of the Democratic Party have not only failed to condemn the bigotry of some of the Party's newest elected officials, but have both defended them and vilified those who stood up and protested — such as President Trump. And public support for Democrats has remained strong.

Combining the sociologists' results and Rabbi Sacks' admonition, it is clear which side of America's acrimonious divide is actually reducing hate — and which side urgently needs to clean house.

Rabbi Yaakov Menken is the Managing Director of the Coalition for Jewish Values. Clarence Henderson, a veteran of the 1960's Woolworth's Sit-in Movement, is President of the Frederick Douglass Foundation of North Carolina, a church elder, and public speaker.

Opinion

TRUMP GIVES BLACK AMERICANS OPPORTUNITY FOR GREATNESS
PRESIDENT'S POLICIES PAY DIVIDENDS FOR SUCCESS

Published Wednesday, July 17, 2019

By Clarence Henderson

Support independent local journalism. Subscribe to the Charlotte Post

While the mainstream media and Democratic establishment smear President Trump, he's busy implementing policies that benefit all Americans. When he arrives in Greenville for a massive campaign rally this week, the President will bring with him a record that promises a new deal for black America.

Black voters understand that the divide-and-conquer strategy pursued by the Democrats is no longer in their interest. The African American community needs opportunity, employment, and a fair deal — not racial pandering, group division, and dependency-inducing handouts that the Democrats have been using to purloin our votes for 50 years.

But Democrats have nothing else to offer: too afraid to take on their elite patrons who promote race-based political correctness, Democratic politicians choose to spew divisive rhetoric rather than enact concrete change, and use welfare payments as tools to maintain the economic status quo.

Instead of handouts and slogans, black America needs structural reforms and access to greater opportunity. President Trump has pushed for these changes in his ongoing fight to bring back the American jobs lost to outsourcing and restore genuine economic potential to low-income communities, and he will undoubtedly make his success on that front a focal point of his rally in Greenville on Wednesday.

For decades, the establishment elites exported American jobs overseas and imported cheap foreign labor. Working Americans of all colors paid the price, forced to support their families with dwindling chances for real advancement. American wages remained stagnant, unemployment stayed high, and economic growth slowed to a crawl.

African American communities bore a disproportionately heavy portion of the burden, enduring persistently high poverty, unemployment, and crime rates because so many opportunities had been taken away by elitist greed.

The Democrat politicians who claim to speak for African Americans have offered us little more than the crumbs from their table. Instead of addressing the hostile economic conditions holding black Americans back, Democrats always try to deflect criticism from their own failed policies by calling conservatives racists. Many black "leaders" actively participate in this deception, exploiting our suffering to enrich them-selves and win phony praise from America's upper crust.

All the while, America's ruling class has cynically used the rich legacy of the Civil Rights Movement to advance its own elitist agenda, leveraging heroic protests such as the Greensboro sit-in — which I proudly took part in — to pass transgender bathroom bills.

Thanks to President Trump's America First economic policies, though, a new day has dawned, and African Americans are finally being offered genuine opportunity rather than more dependency politics. Instead of paying off the people who have been hurt by globalization with government welfare checks, as the Democrats often promise to do, President Trump has taken on elite interests and completely rewritten the rules of the game. With President Trump, working Americans have a champion in Washington who will defend their interests and give them the fair deal they so desperately need.

Black Americans have already begun to see the gains, achieving our lowest unemployment rate ever recorded and benefiting from the rejuvenated wage growth that Trump's pro-growth policies have brought about. The progress African Americans have made under the Trump administration has proven Frederick Douglass correct: we don't need Democrats to take care of us, we need to be left alone.

"You're doing with them is their greatest misfortune," Douglass once advised political leaders who were debating what to do with the soon-to-be-emancipated slaves. "They have been undone by your doings, and all they now ask, and really have need of at your hands, is just to let them alone. They suffer by every interference, and succeed best by being let alone."

African Americans don't need Democrats turning us into victims. Though we may have suffered grave injustices in the past, we don't need white liberals to take care of us. We're perfectly capable of making a better future for ourselves; we just need the freedom and the opportunity to take care of ourselves and our own. President Trump's policies, which are designed to unleash the full potential of the American people, are enabling the African American community to stand tall on its own two feet.

Democrats see that the Trump economy has provided success and opportunity to people whose votes they have long taken for granted, and they're clearly starting to get worried. In response, they have ramped up the racially-divisive rhetoric in order to create irrational fear of Donald Trump among the very people who are benefiting the most from his policies. We can't let the left foil the president's plans to guide the American economy to even greater heights, and that means call-ing them out for their despicable race-baiting and name calling. While Democrats often claim to speak for black America, they're really moti-vated solely by their own interests.

When he visits North Carolina, a place that played a critical role in the historic beginnings of the Civil Rights Movement, President Trump will celebrate the new possibilities that his policies are opening up for all Americans. In doing so, he offers the promise of a new shared future, realizing the goals that the Civil Rights Movement only dared to dream. Under this president's leadership, American workers pursue their dreams with confidence that their government puts them first, irrespective of their race or creed. Under these conditions, black Americans can look forward to a future of accomplishment and prosperity.

Clarence Henderson is president of the Frederick Douglass Foundation of North Carolina, which champions conservative values.

Conservative radio host Glenn Beck leads All Lives Matter march through Birmingham

Published: Aug. 29, 2015 at 10:36 PM EDT | Updated: Sep. 5, 2015 at 10:36 PM EDT

BIRMINGHAM, AL (WBRC) - The streets of downtown Birmingham have been the stage for movements that spark change.

It's why the popular conservative radio personality Glenn Beck brought his movement and message to the Magic City Saturday morning.

A crowd that spanned as far as the eye could see marched the same route civil right leader Dr. Martin Luther King Jr. once walked.

They held signs that read "love one another" and "God is the answer" and chanted "all lives matter"

The event drew hundreds, if not thousands, from different corners of U.S. and from all walks of life

The march is part of a weekend of events hosted by Beck.

According to his website, Never Again Is Now is a movement to stop injustice in the world and references people in the Middle East who are being persecuted for their beliefs and faith.

Matt Hoss traveled from Missouri with his two teenage sons to be a part of what he hopes is history.

"Take off and the whole world to take a stand like we're doing here today," Hoss explained.

Glenn Beck leads All Lives Matter march through Birmingham

Gayle Snead, and his wife who traveled from Texas, says he was inspired by the large crowd and wants to see beck's message of unity take off too.

"And we were enjoying it and having a good time because we have to come together. Now is the time," Snead said.

Copyright 2015 WBRC. All rights reserved.

Chapter 9

OUR TIME AT THE WHITE HOUSE

MY WIFE, ROBIN and I were extremely elated to have been invited to Christmas receptions at the White House in 2017 and 2020. Neither of us would have ever thought about or dreamed of this occurring in either of our lives. We do not take our lives for granted and are thankful to God for the opportunities that have been presented to us along this journey. We will continue to work diligently for causes that affect our lives as Christian Americans and look forward to all that is in store for us as God leads us into the future. And to that we say "To God be the Glory!"

White House Christmas December 2017

White House Christmas December 2020

Chapter 10

A CALL TO ACTION

IN THESE PRECARIOUS times, We the People have been called to defend our freedom just as those of generations past. During this time, I request a specific "Call to Action" that is required to defend our freedom and to remind you that our freedom must be defended at all times understanding that freedom is not free. There is a price to be paid. It must be paid in full and it must be paid up front.

Ronald Reagan stated that "Freedom is never more than one generation away from extinction. We didn't pass it to our children in the bloodstream. It must be fought for, protected, and handed on for them to do the same, or one day we will spend our sunset years telling our children and our children's children what it was once like in the United States where men were free."

And so, today in the year 2022, people are being canceled. Their lives are being destroyed simply because of someone's perception and not reality.

This perception is based on their created concept of racism, privilege, or any other emotion that has caused them to lose their common sense. They are doing this to cancel freedoms of religion, speech, and anything else they may not agree with.

We must tear down the left leaning wall of Socialism, Communism, Marxism and any kind of ism except Capitalism.

We must do our part to win our local elections, no matter what the odds. We must always understand that elections have consequences.

Far too many people in America have cut their teeth on the com-fort of security and far too few have cut their teeth on the true grit of courage that is required for the sake of freedom.

Fortunately there are organizations like the Frederick Douglass Foundation of North Carolina that are at the forefront of defending America's freedom based on the self-evident truth that we all are created equal and have been endowed by our Creator with certain unalienable rights and among them are life, liberty and the pursuit of happiness as stated in the Declaration of Independence.

As one of those who has gone through and continues to reach back to share what I went through to carry others over, I am asking you to join me today, at this, our modern day lunch counter and sit down to stand up for freedom.

EXCERPTS FROM SPEECHES

Freedom's Requirement

When in the course of human events we find ourselves being governed by the rule of man rather than the rule of law, we as sovereign citizens must defend our Charters of Freedom - Declaration of Independence, Constitution, and Bill of Rights.

We must remain one nation under God, with liberty and justice for all. We must live out our motto, "In God we trust."

"We must hold on to the self-evident truth that all men are created equal, that they are endowed by their Creator with certain unalienable Rights, that these are Life, Liberty and the pursuit of Happiness, -- That to secure these rights, Governments are instituted among Men, deriving their just powers from the governed ..." (and not the government). ...

Let My People Go

On February 1st 1960 a shot was fired that was heard around the world when four students walked into F. W. Woolworths in downtown Greensboro, N.C. and sat down at their lunch counter and asked to be served. It was not anything unusual, or it should not have been, except these four students were black and they sat down where the code of law known as Jim Crow forbade them to do so.

Why did these four Moses part the Red Sea of segregation? Why did these four Daniels' go into the lion's den of oppression? Why did these four Hebrew's cross the color line and step over into the fiery furnace of hatred? Why? I'll tell you why, to tell ole Jim Crow to Let my people go. ...

Made in the USA
Columbia, SC
21 February 2025

9f53dbee-8a28-4234-bd7c-9de49a520e54R01